Abstract

In this paper we examine troubled banks—those that receive a poor safety-and-soundness rating when examined—in order to predict future bank state. Besides failure, we see three alternative outcomes for these banks: recovery, acquisition, or continuation as a problem. The determinants of bank failure have been much researched, as has failure prediction. Most of this research uses a binary approach, dividing banks into two groups (those that fail and those that do not) or predicting one of two states (failure or nonfailure). Because our sample contains only troubled banks, we can go beyond a two-state approach.

First we use univariate trend analysis to determine whether financial variables differ within this group of banks depending on the banks' future states. This analysis suggests that meaningful relationships exist between these future states and prior-period financial conditions. We then use financial ratios as explanatory variables in a unified model of bank states, with the goal of improving predictions of future bank condition.

We gauge the model's effectiveness by testing the out-of-sample forecasting accuracy. Our results show that our model compares favorably with the standard binary failure-prediction model, yet has the added feature of predicting recovery, merger, or continuation as a problem bank.

1. Introduction

A wealth of literature exists examining the determinants of bank failures and bank mergers and acquisitions. Also numerous are studies developing failure-prediction models and early-warning systems. Because these studies use samples of all banks, most of this research focuses on pairs of outcomes: failure versus nonfailure, merger versus acquisition, or problem banks versus nonproblem banks.

In this paper, we contribute to this literature by studying only troubled banks—banks that receive a composite CAMELS rating of either 4 or 5 when examined.[1] Focusing on troubled banks is especially valuable for four reasons. First, for troubled banks, failure is but one possible outcome. Alternative outcomes include recovery, acquisition, or continuation as a problem. Second, between 1990 and 2002, 96 percent of all banks that failed had first been troubled banks. Third, the number of troubled banks rose in the period 1999 through 2002 but began to decrease in 2003. This uptick is especially important to the Federal Deposit Insurance Corporation (FDIC), whose mission is to protect depositors and promote the safety and soundness of insured depository institutions and the U.S. financial system by identifying, monitoring, and addressing risks to the deposit insurance funds. The Financial Risk Committee within the FDIC quantifies risks to the deposit insurance system for purposes of financial reporting and fund management. Each quarter, the committee meets to set a contingent loss reserve estimated from total assets of banks that may fail within two years. The ability to better predict the number of troubled banks that will not fail would improve the committee's estimates for the contingent loss reserve.

---

[1] CAMELS is an acronym for the five components of the regulatory rating system: Capital adequacy , Asset quality, Management, Earnings, Liquidity, and market Sensitivity. Examiners have rated sensitivity only since 1998. Banks with a rating of 4 or 5 are considered problem banks. Four-rated banks generally exhibit unsafe or unsound practices or condition, while 5-rated banks exhibit extremely unsafe or unsound practices or condition.

Finally, developing a multistate model identifying financial characteristics that contribute to recovery as well as to failure is important for the FDIC's long-term strategic planning. Accurate predictions of the future states of problem banks would affect the resources applied to these banks.

Knowing the future states of banks in our sample, we construct financial profiles for each of the four groups. We then use these profiles to develop a multinomial logit estimating procedure that predicts the likelihood of a bank's future state: recovery, acquisition, continuation as a problem, or failure.[2] We show that a four-state model predicts at least as well as binary failure-prediction models and adds predictive ability for alternative future states.

The next section of this study describes previous empirical studies of bank failures, mergers, and financial distress. Section 3 discusses our methodology; section 4, our sample and data; section 5, our results; and section 6 concludes.

2. Empirical Studies

Studies examining the determinants of bank failures and bank mergers and acquisitions are numerous. Also numerous are studies developing early-warning systems predicting deterioration in banks' financial condition.[3] Most of the work in this literature constructs financial ratios taken from the Consolidated Reports of Condition and Income (Call Reports) that banks file quarterly with the FDIC. The idea is to construct financial ratios that closely resemble the CAMELS rating system used by bank examiners to predict pairs of outcomes: failure versus nonfailure, mergers versus acquirers, or problem banks versus nonproblem banks. (See Whalen [1991]; Cole and Gunther [1998]; Kolari et al. [2002]; and Jagtiani et al. [2003].)

---

[2] Because of the nature of the resolution process, we deliberately omit troubled thrifts, including those resolved by the Resolution Trust Corporation, which kept insolvent thrifts open while trying to close them.

[3] For reviews of the literature, see Demirgüç-Kunt (1989); Jagtiani et al. (2003); and King et al. (2005).

Only a few studies have extended this research beyond pairs of outcomes. In an effort to improve predictive accuracy, DeYoung (2003) estimates the long-run probability of failure and acquisition in de novo banks by defining three states: (1) failure, (2) merger by acquisition, and (3) conversion of a whole-bank affiliate of a bank holding company to a branch bank of that bank holding company. Wheelock and Wilson (2000) use a competing-risks model to consider explicitly the joint determination of the probability of being acquired, failing, or surviving. Hannan and Rhoades (1987) predict that a bank may experience one of three outcomes: (1) not be acquired, (2) be acquired by a firm operating within its market, or (3) be acquired by a firm operating outside its market. DeYoung expects that including the other two exit states (merger by acquisition, and conversion) will improve the accuracy of the failure estimates. Wheelock and Wilson find that inefficiency increases the risk of failure while reducing the probability of a bank's being acquired. And Hannan and Rhoades find that adding the third state (distinguishing between merger types) yields a number of firm and market characteristics that significantly influence the likelihood of acquisitions—characteristics that earlier studies did not yield.

We add to this literature in two ways. First, because our sample is troubled banks instead of all banks, we can introduce three alternatives to failure: recovery, merger, or continuation as a problem. Second, by adding an additional state to the three-state models above, we hope to improve predictive accuracy for failed banks and add predictions for three outcomes that are alternatives to failure.

3. Methodology

Referencing previous studies, we select certain financial variables proven to be useful in determining future bank state. We use univariate trend analysis to determine whether prior-period financial characteristics differ by future banks' states.

Prior literature on bank performance suggests a number of reasons for failure: low earnings, low liquidity, risky asset portfolios, and poor management, to name a few. Thus we select financial variables from the same broad categories used to explain or predict binary bank states: capital adequacy, asset quality, management, earnings, and liquidity. In addition, we run a one-way analysis of variance to examine the financial characteristics of recovered banks versus banks in the other three states.

We use a multinomial logistic estimating procedure to model future bank state. Outcomes are nominal, and therefore the multinomial logit model's assumptions are the closest fit to the specification of the model being estimated. This model simultaneously estimates binary logits for pairwise comparisons among the outcome categories to a reference outcome. These binary logits are (1) recover relative to failure, (2) merge relative to failure, and (3) remain a problem relative to failure.

A general form of the model tested is shown in equation 1, where *Probability of State* $(k)_{i,t}$ is the probability that bank i will be in state k at time t.

(1)   *Probability of State* $(k)_{i,t} = F(Financial\ condition_{i,t-1},\ Economic\ conditions_t)$

We gauge the model's effectiveness in several ways. First, we compare the out-of-sample forecasting accuracy for each of the four states with the actual number of banks ending up in each state. Two competing binary models are compared with the multistate model for failure predictions, one that uses the same variables that our multistate model uses and a second that uses the same explanatory variables that Jarrow et al. (2003) used, referred to as the loss-distribution model. These two comparisons allow us to test whether including additional alternative states improves the accuracy of failure estimates over binary models. Second, we investigate the economic and statistical effect of our explanatory variables. Third, we check to determine that the banks with the highest predicted probability of failure from our model are the ones that actually fail.

4.   Sample and Data

Our sample consists of 1,996 banks on the FDIC problem-bank list from 1990 through 2002. Each bank has at least one first event and second event that are paired as an observation. The first event occurs when a bank is examined and receives a CAMELS rating of 4 or 5. The second event occurs when the bank (1) recovers—improves to a CAMELS rating of 1, 2, or 3 at the next examination, (2) merges—either merges with a bank outside of its multibank holding company or consolidates within its multibank holding company,[4] (3) remains a problem bank—continues to have a CAMELS rating of 4 or 5 at the next examination, or (4) fails.[5] We use only observations in which first events are paired with second events that occurred 6 to 24 months after the first events. (Any second events sooner than 6 months or later than 24 months are ignored, and the observation is dropped from the sample.) The reason for this restriction is twofold: first, we want to allow enough time to pass for changes in financial condition to occur;

---

[4] We recognize that characteristics differ between mergers and consolidations. However, during this period, the number of consolidations is small (39). Because of the small number, we combined both events into one state.
[5] In the paper, failure is defined either as a closing that results from an action by a regulator or as a merger assisted by the FDIC.

6

second, examination frequency set by the Federal Deposit Insurance Corporation Improvement Act of 1991 (FDICIA) was in effect during most of our period. FDICIA requires annual safety-and-soundness examinations except for banks with assets under $250 million and a composite CAMELS rating of 1 or 2. (Further exceptions may be found in the act.) As noted above, a pairing of events is considered one observation in our sample. Our sample consists of 3,747 observations.

We divide these observations into annual cohorts corresponding to the year of the first event to allow us to implicitly control for the effects of economic conditions and banking legislation. Because second events usually occur in a year different from the first event, we recognize that using annual cohorts does not completely control for these effects.

A bank appears as an observation in a cohort only once, and each observation belongs to only one cohort.[6] All observations end with the occurrence of the second event. If the bank in a given cohort reaches the second event as recovered (or merged, or a continued problem), the outcome for the observation for that bank in the cohort is considered a recovery (or a merger, or continuation as a problem).

The same bank can be an observation in multiple cohorts depending on when it first receives a CAMELS rating of 4 or 5 and on its outcome at the second event (continuation as a problem vis-à-vis recovery or merger). The repeat appearance of a bank in a subsequent cohort occurs with the second event when the bank, upon reexamination, continues as a problem bank. For such banks, the first observation ends with an outcome of continuation as a problem bank. Concurrently a second observation for that bank begins and is paired with its corresponding subsequent event, which takes place 6 to 24 months later. At this subsequent event, an outcome

---

[6] Technically a bank may appear as a second observation in the same cohort since the window for the second event is as short as 6 months.

is determined for that second observation. In contrast, a bank that recovers or merges at the second event has no concurrent second observation since it is no longer a problem bank. However, recovered banks may reemerge in our sample in a later cohort (for example, the bank recovers but later reverts to problem-bank status) following the recovery, whereupon the bank would be considered a new observation. Banks cannot appear in cohorts after they fail.

Our sample has the following characteristics: The number of problem banks declines drastically during the 1990s as the banking crisis that began in the mid-1980s and lasted through the early 1990s subsided. As figure 1 shows, the 1991 cohort has the highest number—897; the 1997 cohort has the lowest number—62. Both the 1990 and 1998 cohorts have the highest percentage of problem banks that fail—5 percent. No problem banks fail before the second event in the 1997 or 2002 cohorts. (See figure 2.) Most remain a problem at the second event, ranging from a high of 69 percent in the 1990 cohort to a low of 40 percent in the 1997 cohort, with an average of 49 percent. The proportion that merge by the second event is small, ranging from 3 percent in the 1990 cohort to 20 percent in the 1998 cohort. The proportion that recover by the second event ranges from a low of 23 percent in the 1990 cohort to a high of 53 percent in the 1997 cohort. [7] Figure 3 shows that most banks that remain a problem at the second event ultimately recover. [8]

Using data from the Call Reports, we calculate beginning and ending periods for each bank. The beginning period is calculated from the Call Report filed just before the first event

---

[7] Jones and Critchfield (2004) note three reasons that might explain the 1997 and 1998 peak years for merger activity and recoveries: (1) banks were highly profitable, liquid, and operating in favorable economic and interest-rate environments; (2) the Riegle-Neal Interstate Banking and Branching Efficiency Act of 1994 removed the remaining barriers to interstate banking and branching; and (3) a record-breaking bull market in stocks pushed market valuations of banks and thrifts to unprecedented levels, encouraging many banking firms to use their stock as currency to purchase other firms. Moreover, we found large increases in internal capital injections (as a percent of average assets) for banks that recovered peaked in 1996. External capital injections increased sharply from 1994 to 1995 but did not peak until 1999. (See figure 4.)

[8] The reason for the decline in the percentage of still-a-problem banks that ultimately recover beginning in 2001 is that enough follow-up events have not yet occurred. Most banks remain a problem beyond a second event.

and the one filed 12 months previously.[9] Balance-sheet items are averaged for the two reporting periods and taken as a ratio of average assets for the same two periods; income items are summed over the 12-month period and taken as a percentage of average assets for the two periods. Similar calculations are made for the ending period, using the Call Report filed immediately before the second event and the one filed 12 months previously.

We group banks by future state to compare their condition and performance. We then compare data reported at the ending period with those reported for the beginning. We compute the percentage of banks in each state with an increase between the two periods for each of the financial ratios. Assuming that banks that recover are able to improve net income and net noninterest income more than those that fail, we expect to see that the percentages of banks with increases in such ratios will be greater for banks having a future state of recovery than for banks with a future state of failure. For expense items, we expect the opposite. Assuming that banks that recover shed nonperforming and past-due assets, we expect that the percentages of banks with increases in such assets will be less for banks that recover than for those that fail. We expect that the percentages of banks with increases in volatile liabilities and illiquid assets will be smaller for banks having a future state of recovery than for banks with a future state of failure, and that the percentages of banks with increases in capital will be larger for banks that recover than for those that fail. We have no expectations for the ranking of banks that merge or are still a problem except that the percentages that increase will lie between the percentages for banks that recover and banks that fail.

---

[9] Gunther and Moore (2000) find atypical movements in Call Report data for the quarters in which banks are downgraded by examiners. These Call Reports are more subject to revisions. For that reason, we also did our univariate analysis on the Call Reports filed before the ones specified in this paper. The resulting trends in data were similar to the trends reported in this paper.

We compare the percentages of banks in each state with increases in net interest income, provision for loan losses, and net noninterest income as measures of earnings; average allowance for loan and lease losses, average loans and leases past due 30–89 days, average loans and leases past due 90 days or more, average nonaccrual loans and leases, and average other real estate owned as measures of risky asset portfolios; average risk-based capital and average tangible equity capital as measures of capital adequacy; average volatile liabilities and loans and securities with maturities greater than or equal to five years as measures for liquidity; and for the management measure, we use the efficiency ratio (noninterest expense as a percentage of net interest income plus noninterest income). A lower efficiency ratio is better.

To model future bank states, we select almost the same financial variables that were used in the univariate trend analysis.[10] We added capital injections from a bank holding company and capital injections from outside as measures of the economy.[11] From the univariate trend analysis we are able to form expectations concerning the sign that coefficients on these variables will take when estimated using logit analysis. A negative coefficient implies that an increase in the variable will result in the future state's becoming less likely relative to failure. A positive coefficient implies the opposite.

Table 1 shows the expected sign of explanatory variables used in the multistate model. As table 1 shows, the financial ratios associated with not failing are capital, capital injections, allowance for loan losses, interest income, noninterest income, and longer-term assets (assets and securities with maturities equal to or great than five years). Although we expect a negative sign

---

[10] For the logits we used total income and detailed expense items instead of net interest and net noninterest income as used in the univariate analysis. In addition, we also estimated the model using Call Report data from the quarter before the quarter that precedes the examination, as in the univariate. The results differed little from those reported in this paper.

[11] As noted in footnote 6, the economy (a record-breaking bull market) was one reason noted for increased acquisitions.

for the efficiency ratio's coefficient (because lower is better), we also associate this ratio with not failing. The financial ratios associated with failure are those measuring poor asset quality (past-due loans, nonaccruing loans, and real estate owned), expense items (interest expense, loss provision, loan charge-offs, salaries, expenses on premises, and other noninterest expense), and volatile liquidity as measured by volatile liabilities.[12]

5. Results

Our results from both the univariate trend analysis and the multistate logit estimating procedure are generally in agreement with expectations. The percentage of banks with increases (between the beginning and ending periods) in performance ratios such as net income and net noninterest income that recover is greater than the percentage in any alternative state. For loan loss provisions, the opposite occurs. In addition, the percentage of banks that have increases in any of the risky asset measures and recover is less than the percentage in any alternative state.

In the logit analysis, we find that increases in financial ratios associated with nonfailure have positive coefficients, and those associated with failure have negative coefficients.

5.1 Univariate Trend Analysis

For all three earnings measures, the relative position of banks that recover is the best; and the position of banks that fail is the worst. As shown in figure 5, 62 percent of banks that recover (825 banks) have an increase in net interest income between the beginning and ending periods, compared with 28 percent of banks that fail (33 banks). The percentages for banks that

---

[12] Volatile liabilities are federal funds purchased and sold under agreements to repurchase, demand notes issued to the U.S. Treasury and other borrowed money, time deposits over $100,000 held in domestic offices, foreign office deposits, trading liabilities less trading liabilities' revaluation losses on interest rate, foreign exchange rate, and other commodity and equity contracts.

merge or are still a problem are also greater than the percentage for those that fail, but less than that for those that recover. A similar trend is seen for net noninterest income (figure 6). Fifty-two percent of banks (689 banks) that recover experience an increase in net noninterest income, compared with 32 percent of banks that fail (37 banks).

Figure 7 shows that a smaller percentage of banks that recover have an increase in loss provision between the two periods: 28 percent of banks that recover (372 banks) experience an increase in provision for loan losses at the second event, compared with 46 percent of banks that fail (53 banks). The percentages for banks that merge or are still a problem are less than the percentage for those that fail but greater than the percentage for banks that recover.

For all five asset-quality measures, our results agree with our expectations. The relative position of banks that recover is the best; the position of those that fail is the worst. A smaller percentage of banks that recover experience increases in loan-loss reserves, average loans and leases past due 30–89 days, average loans and leases past due 90 days or more, average nonaccrual loans and leases, and average other real estate owned between the beginning and ending periods than banks that merge, remain a problem, or fail. As shown in figure 8, 50 percent of banks that recover (667 banks) experience an increase in loan-loss reserves, compared with 72 percent of banks that fail (84 banks). The percentages for banks that merge or remain a problem are less than the percentage for those that fail but greater than the percentage for banks that recover. Figure 9 shows that 36 percent of banks that recover (476 banks) experience an increase in average loans and leases past due 30–89 days, compared with 56 percent of banks that fail (65 banks). Forty-one percent of banks that recover (543 banks) experience an increase in average loans and leases past due 90 days or more, compared with 56 percent of banks that fail (65 banks), as shown in figure 10. Figure 11 shows that 38 percent of banks that recover

(509 banks) experience an increase in nonaccrual loans and leases, compared with 61 percent of banks that fail (71 banks). Forty-four percent of banks that recover (585 banks) experience an increase in other real estate owned, compared with 76 percent of banks that fail (88 banks), as shown in figure 12.

In line with our expectations, a larger percentage of banks that recover experience increases in average risk-based capital and average tangible equity capital between the beginning and ending periods than banks in any alternative state. The smallest percentage of banks experiencing increases are those that fail. Figure 13 shows that 72 percent of banks that recover (952 banks) experience an increase in average risk-based capital, compared with 14 percent of banks that fail (16 banks). And figure 14 shows that 70 percent of banks that recover (926 banks) experience an increase in average tangible equity capital, compared with 13 percent of banks that fail (15 banks).

In its 1988 study of bank failures, the Office of the Comptroller of the Currency (OCC) lists overreliance on volatile liabilities as one of the root causes of failure. We find, however, that banks that fail have the smallest percentage of banks with an increase in volatile liabilities between the beginning and ending periods. This result could be because management has reduced brokered deposits as required by more recent legislation. (The Federal Deposit Insurance Corporation Improvement Act of 1991 restricts the activities of critically undercapitalized institutions. One such restriction is that these institutions cannot pay an exceptionally large amount of interest on new or renewed liabilities.)

In its 1988 study the OCC also notes that failed banks frequently had inadequate liquid assets as a second source of liquidity. Thus, we expect the percentage of banks that experience an increase in loans and securities with maturities of greater than or equal to five years between the beginning and ending periods to be larger for banks that fail than for banks that recover. And our data support this expectation. One explanation for this trend may be that banks that fail were more likely to take on riskier loans (construction loans, commercial real estate loans) than banks that recover.

Twenty-six percent of banks that recover (351 banks) experience an increase in volatile liabilities, compared with only 19 percent of banks that fail (22 banks), as shown in figure 15. Figure 16 shows that 40 percent of banks that fail (46 banks) experience an increase in loans and securities of longer maturities, compared with 37 percent of banks that recover (492 banks).

A larger percentage of banks that recovered experience improvements in the efficiency ratio between the beginning and ending periods than the percentages of banks that merge, remain a problem, or fail. Fifty-nine percent of banks that recover (832 banks) experience an increase in the efficiency ratio, compared with 22 percent of banks that fail (25 banks), as shown in figure 17.

5.2   Analysis of Variance

Tables 2 and 3 show results from the analysis of variance that complement the above results. Table 2 shows the mean and standard errors for financial variables in each state. Table 3 shows the differences in means and statistical significances for six pairings: (1) recover versus merge, (2) recover versus remain a problem, (3) recover versus fail, (4) remain a problem versus merge, (5) remain a problem versus fail, and (6) merge versus fail. The beginning-period data are used in these tables.

The results reported in table 2 show that the mean values for each financial variable are statistically different from zero at the first event. Further, it shows that the mean values in

14

financial ratios associated with not failing are generally most often larger for banks that recover, merge, or remain a problem than they are for banks that fail. The opposite is true for the mean values in financial ratios associated with failing.

There are three exceptions, however: the mean values for total interest income, total noninterest income, and loans and securities with maturities greater than or equal to five years are largest for banks that fail. These results seem counterintuitive until we consider that banks with a future state of fail probably take on riskier assets that will have higher yields than banks in the alternative states. Banks with riskier assets have a higher probability of failure. Fee income from these riskier assets may have resulted in higher noninterest income. And in banks with a future state of fail, the ratio between loans and securities in the longer-term assets may be geared toward loans that are usually considered riskier than more-liquid securities.

The results reported in table 3 show that except for two variables (capital injections from the bank holding company, and capital injections from outside), the difference in means between banks that recover and those that fail is statistically significant. The differences in means between banks that merge and those that fail and between banks that remain a problem and those that fail are also significant for most variables.

The results from table 3 also indicate that the differences in means between banks that remain a problem and banks that merge and between banks that recover and banks that remain a problem are statistically significant. For the pairing recovery versus merger, fewer variables are statistically different from one another. And for the pairing remain a problem versus merger, even fewer variables are statistically different from one another.

5.3   Logit Analysis

For our multivariate analysis, we rely on a multinomial unordered logit probability model that takes into account all four future bank states. Equation 2 shows the model tested:

(2)   *Probability of State* $(k)_{i,t}$ = *F(Financial condition*$_{i,,t-1}$ *)*

We did not include variables for economic condition in our model for a number of reasons. First, Nuxoll et al. (2003) did not find that state and local economic data contributed to the performance of standard off-site models. Second, much of the literature theorizes that the economy is subsumed in the balance sheet. Thus, any effect of the economy has already shown up in the financial data.[13] And, we included capital injections as a proxy for changes in the economy (see footnote 10).

A stepwise logit estimation procedure is used to identify those terms that have a significant relationship in predicting the likelihood that a bank will end up in one of the states: recover, merge, remain a problem, or fail. The stepwise estimation procedure allows us to include several measure of the same attribute in the logit model, yet isolates the most important factors in terms of predicting state.

---

[13] As a robustness check, we did estimate the model using three variables for the economy: a ratio of the number of problem banks to total number of banks by state, a ratio of the assets of problem banks to total assets by state, and the percentage change in state housing permits. The first test was an estimation using only the economic variables as explanatory variables. We did two estimations: one used the ratio of the number of problem banks to total by state and the percentage change in state housing permits; the second used the ratio of the assets of problem banks to total by state and the percentage change in housing permits. These variables were significant for most of these estimations. However, when they were included in estimations with the rest of the explanatory variables, their significance disappeared.

Table 4 shows summary statistics for the variables used in the logistic regressions. The beginning-period data, as explained in the section on sample and data, are used in this table.[14]

We estimate the logits for each of our cohorts, 1990 through 2002. However, because of the small number of failures, beginning with the 1994 logit we combine cohorts. The 1994 model is a combination of the 1993 and 1994 cohorts, and the 1995 model combines 1993 through 1995. We continue combining cohorts up to five years (the 1993 through 1997 cohorts for the 1997 logit). For the 1998 models through 2002 we use a panel of the most recent previous five years.

Tables 5 through 7 show the results. The reference state is failure, so the coefficients are interpreted relative to failure. As mentioned above, a negative coefficient means that an increase in a variable will have the result that the future state relative to failure becomes less likely.

Some of the more interesting findings are noted here. First, more recent cohorts (beginning with the 1995–99 cohort) have fewer statistically significant variables than those in the early 1990s. This result is most likely because of the small number of failures, despite the paneling of data. The number of failures totaled 7, 7, 8, and 8, respectively, from the 1995–99 cohort through the 1998–02 cohort, compared with 45, 36, and 17, respectively, for the cohorts 1990 through 1992. However, those variables that are statistically significant in the more recent cohorts have the expected sign (as shown in table 1) except for capital injections. For example, in the 1997–01 cohort, expenses on premises is significant and has a negative sign in table 5 (recovery) and table 7 (still a problem). An increase in this variable will have the result that a future state of recovery or continuation as a problem becomes less likely relative to failure. On the other hand, for the cohorts 1994–98 through 1998–02, capital injections from outside are

---

[14] As with the univariate analysis, we also ran the logits using a beginning period one quarter before the quarters specified previously. Little difference in the results was noticeable.

significant but with the unexpected sign for table 6 (merger) and, in two of those four cohorts, for table 5 (recovery). Perhaps the negative sign indicates that the institution is anticipating it will be acquired and either does not or cannot raise capital. As mentioned above, the Riegle-Neal Interstate Banking and Branching Efficiency Act was enacted in 1994.

Second, both the pairing of recovery versus failure (table 5) and the pairing of merger versus failure (table 6) have more statistically significant variables than the pairing of continuation as a problem versus failure (table 7). We expect that banks that remain a problem more closely resemble banks that fail than they resemble banks that recover or merge. In fact, the univariate trend analysis showed that for most of the financial variables, the percentage of banks that remained a problem was closer to the percentage that failed than were the percentages for the remaining two future states.

Third, asset-quality variables in each future state (tables 5, 6, and 7) are more often statistically significant than other variables for each cohort. Moreover, nonaccrual loans and leases is more often statistically significant than past-due loans (either 30–89 days or 90 days or more), a result we would expect inasmuch as past-due loans are more likely to improve and be worked out than nonaccrual loans and leases. Further, these variables are negative (as expected from table 1), indicating that an increase in the variable will have the result that the future state relative to failure becomes less likely.

Fourth, surprisingly, tangible equity is highly statistically significant for only the 1990, 1991, and 1992 cohorts in table 5 (recovery) and table 6 (merger). It is not statistically significant in the remaining years in tables 5 or 6, nor is it significant in any year in table 7 (continuation as a problem).[15]

---

[15] Thinking that tangible equity would be correlated with capital injections, we ran the models using only tangible equity. However, taking out capital injections made no difference in significance.

Fifth, another surprise is in the 1992 cohort, where external capital injections are significant and positive for all three future states (and yet are not significant again until the 1994–98 cohort for merger [table 6], where the sign is negative).

Sixth, the efficiency ratio is significant only for the 1991 cohort for continuation as a problem versus failure (table 7). Since it is a ratio using income and expense variables, we omitted the earnings variables from the model as a robustness check. The results showed that without the earnings variables, the frequency of significance improved in the efficiency ratio. For example, in the 1993–97 and 1994–98 cohorts, the efficiency ratio is significant in all three future states and has the expected sign. In the 1991 and 1992 cohorts, it is significant for recovery versus failure and has the expected sign.

Seventh, in the earnings ratios, loan-loss provision is the most consistently significant ratio in all three future states, but more so for recovery (table 5) than for the other two outcomes (table 6 and table 7). This result makes sense since the sooner loan losses are recognized, the more likely it is that a bank will survive. We also tried running the logits without the efficiency ratio to see whether we could gain more significance in the earnings ratios. However, the significance in the earnings ratios still did not become more frequent.

Finally, the most startling result is in the 1994–98 cohort for all three future states. The coefficients for loans past due 90 days, nonaccrual loans and leases, and other real estate owned are much larger than in any other cohorts, and the sign on other real estate owned is positive (indicating that an increase in this variable is more likely to result in nonfailure). The likely explanation is the small number of failures and the banks that are in the 1994–98 cohort. First, the number of failures fell from 10 in the 1993–97 cohort to 7 in the 1994–98 cohort. Second, one of the failures included in 1998 was a bank that failed because of fraudulent activity. As a

19

result, this bank had a very low amount of other real estate owned, perhaps enough to skew the model. For example, the mean of other real estate owned (as a percentage of assets) for failed banks in the 1993–97 cohort equaled 3.0 percent; for the 1994–98 cohort the mean dropped to 0.62 percent.

5.4   Prediction of State: Out-of-Sample Results

Whether the logit model is accurate in making out-of-sample predictions is the true measure of its contribution. To test its accuracy, we forecast future bank states using prior-period estimations from our unordered logit model on the following year's cohort. For example, we use the coefficients from the 1990 cohort to predict the future state of the 1991 cohort, coefficients from the 1991 cohort to predict the future state of the 1992 cohort, and so on. Since our model is estimated from paired observations of first events and outcomes at second events, no observations that are in the 1990 cohort can be in the 1991 cohort (see explanation of observations in the section on sample and data). All state predictions are determined by summing predicted state probabilities for the cohort, yielding the expected number of banks in each future state. Figures 18 through 20 show the results.

All three figures show that the number of predicted banks in each state is very close to the number of actual banks ending up in the state. For example, in figure 18, the logit predicts 27 banks to recover in 1996, and 26 banks actually recovered. Five banks are predicted to be acquired in 1996 (figure 19), compared with 3 that actually merged. And 26 banks are predicted to remain a problem in 1996 (figure 20), compared with 29 that actually did remain problems.

To compare binary forecasts against our multistate model, we do two comparisons. First, we run a binary model using the same financial variables as in the multistate model to predict

20

failure versus nonfailure. We then compare the predicted probabilities of failure from this binary model with predicted probabilities of failure from the multistate model. Figure 21 compares the forecasts of the two models with the actual number of failed banks. As can be seen, both models predict failure fairly accurately.

The second comparison is shown in figure 22. We compare the predicted probabilities of failure from our multistate model with predictions from the loss-distribution model (LDM). This model uses variables found in conventional bank-failure literature to predict bank failure within the second quarter after the Call Report is filed. In our test, we use the betas from the LDM estimated one year earlier to predict failures of problem banks for the following year. For example, the LDM predicted that eight banks would fail in 1994 (figure 22). The predictions resulted from the use of the betas estimated in the 1993 LDM.

As noted above in the section on sample and data, a second event for an observation may occur as many as 24 months after the first event. A bank on the problem list in December 1993 may be in our 1992 cohort that used Call Data after 1993 in the estimation. Thus, to get a true out-of-sample prediction using our model, we have to use the estimated betas from a cohort two years before the date for which we are predicting failures for problem banks. The six banks that are predicted to fail in 1994 resulted from using estimated betas from our 1992 model (figure 22). But since the LDM requires only a one-year prediction horizon, one would expect it to be a better predictor of failure than our model. This expectation is not quite borne out. As figure 22 shows, the two models are comparable. The advantage of ours is that we can predict not only problem-bank failure but also recoveries, mergers, and continuations as problems.

To determine whether banks with the highest probability of failure are the ones that actually fail, we rank banks that our model predicts to fail in each period by their probability of failure. We then divide them into deciles to determine that the highest decile contains the largest number of banks that actually failed. Thirty-eight of the 65 failed banks in our cohorts from 1991 through 2002 were in the tenth decile.[16] An additional 8 banks were in the ninth decile.

The results for the remaining three states, however, were not quite as accurate. Of the 1,058 recovered banks in our cohorts from 1991 through 2002, 166 (16 percent) were in the tenth decile; adding the 159 banks in the ninth decile raises the percentage to 31. For banks that are predicted to merge, 14 percent are in the tenth decile (26 banks out of the 191 banks that merged in our cohorts from 1991 through 2002); and for banks that are predicted to remain a problem, 15 percent are in the tenth decile.

5.5   Economic Significance

To test the economic significance of the explanatory variables, we use a fairly standard approach—evaluating in-sample predicted state probabilities on the basis of the mean values of explanatory variables and evaluating how these probabilities change with marginal changes in key explanatory variables. Because asset-quality variables, specifically loans past due 90 days or more and nonaccrual loans and leases, were the variables most consistently significant across panels, we compared their economic significance in two periods: 1990 and the panel 1995–99.

We use the predicted in-sample state probabilities for 1990 and the 1995–99 panel based on the mean values for explanatory variables in 1990 and in the 1995–99 panel. The means for the sample of banks used in model estimation for both periods are shown in table 8.

The predicted state probabilities evaluated at the mean for banks in the 1990 cohort are 16.41 percent for recover, 1.82 percent for merge, 80.82 percent for remain a problem, and 0.95 percent for fail. Both loans past due 90 days or more and nonaccrual loans and leases were

---

[16] For the binary model, 39 of the 65 failed banks were in the tenth decile.

statistically significant in 1990 and in the 1995–99 panel. Table 9 shows the effects on estimated state probabilities, ceteris paribus, should each of these ratios experience a 1 percentage point increase in either of the periods examined. For example, in 1990 the mean for loans past due 90 days or more equaled 0.7964 percent of assets. If that is increased 1 percentage point to 1.7964 percent, the probability of recovery decreases from 16.41 percent to 12.52 percent; the probability of merger decreases from 1.82 percent to 1.59 percent; the probability of continuation as a problem increases from 80.82 percent to 84.74 percent; and the probability of failure increases from 0.95 percent to 1.15 percent.

6.   Conclusions

We offer an approach that differs from that of previous failure-prediction models. Because we focus on troubled banks only, we can estimate a model to predict failures and the three alternative outcomes: recovery, merger and continuation as a problem.

Our results show that our model not only compares favorably with the standard binary failure-prediction model but also gives banks that will eventually fail the highest probability of failure. Further, the explanatory variables are economically significant.

Knowing these four predicted states is arguably more helpful to the deposit insurer than knowing only two predicted states. First, the FDIC's long-term strategic planning requires knowing the likely direction of all problem banks; second, bank regulation often focuses on whether policy can affect the likelihood that troubled banks can successfully resolve their own problems.

References

Demirgüç-Kunt, Asli. 1989. Deposit-Institution Failures: A Review of the Empirical Literature. Federal Reserve Bank of Cleveland *Economic Review* (Quarter 4): 2–18.

DeYoung, Robert. 2003. De Novo Bank Exit. *Journal of Money, Credit, and Banking* 35, no. 5:711–28.

Cole, Rebel A., and Jeffery W. Gunther. 1998. Predicting Bank Failures: A Comparison of On- and Off-Site Monitoring Systems. *Journal of Financial Services Research* 13, no. 2:103–17.

Hannan, Timothy H., and Stephen A. Rhoades. 1987. Acquisition Targets and Motives: The Case of the Banking Industry. *Review of Economics and Statistics* 69, no. 1:67–74.

Gunther, Jeffery W., and Robert R. Moore. 2000. Financial Statements and Reality: Do Troubled Banks Tell All?. Federal Reserve Bank of Dallas *Economic and Financial Review* (Quarter 3): 30–35.

Jagtiani, Julapa, James Kolari, Catharine Lemieux, and Hwan Shin. 2003. Early Warning Models for Bank Supervision: Simpler Could Be Better. Federal Reserve Bank of Chicago *Economic Perspectives* (Quarter 3): 49–60.

Jarrow, Robert A., Rosalind L. Bennett, Michael C. Fu, Daniel A. Nuxoll, and Huiju Zhang. 2003. A General Martingale Approach to Measuring and Valuing the Risk to the FDIC Deposit Insurance Funds. Unpublished paper, presented at the FDIC Conference on Finance and Banking: New Perspectives.

Jones, Kenneth D., and Tim Critchfield. 2004. The Declining Number of U.S. Banking Organizations: Will the Trend Continue? Future of Banking Study. Online. FDIC. Available at: http://www.fdic.gov/bank/analytical/future/index.html. March 11, 2005.

King, Thomas B., Andrew P. Meyer, Daniel A. Nuxoll, and Timothy J. Yeager. Are the Causes of Bank Distress Changing? Can Researchers Keep Up? Center for Financial Research Working Paper Series, no. 2005-03. FDIC.

Kolari, James, Dennis Glennon, Hwan Shin, and Michele Caputo. 2002. Predicting Large U.S. Commercial Bank Failures. *Journal of Economic and Business* 54:361–87.

Nuxoll, Daniel A., John O'Keefe, and Katherine Samolyk. 2003. Do Local Economic Data Improve Off-Site Bank-Monitoring Models? FDIC *Banking Review* 15, no. 2:39–53.

Whalen, Gary. 1991. A Proportional Hazard Model of Bank Failure: An Examination of Its Usefulness as an Early Warning Tool. Federal Reserve Bank of Cleveland *Economic Review* 27, no. 1:21–31.

Wheelock, David C., and Paul W. Wilson. 2000. Why do Banks Disappear? The Determinants of U.S. Bank Failures and Acquisitions. *Review of Economics and Statistics* 82, no. 1:127–38.

Figure 1
Number of Troubled Banks by Cohort

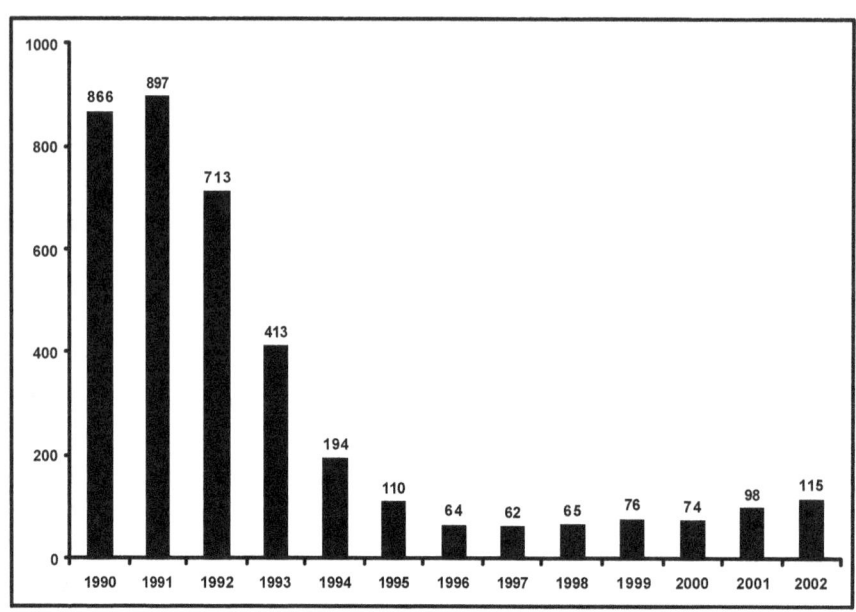

Figure 2
Cohort Composition of Troubled Banks at Second Event

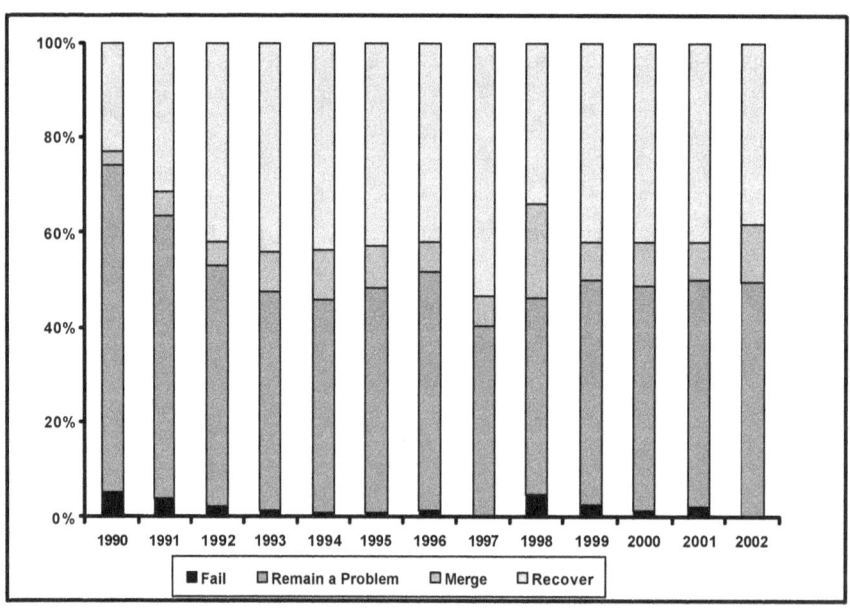

Figure 3
Number of Troubled Banks That
Remain a Problem and Ultimately Recover

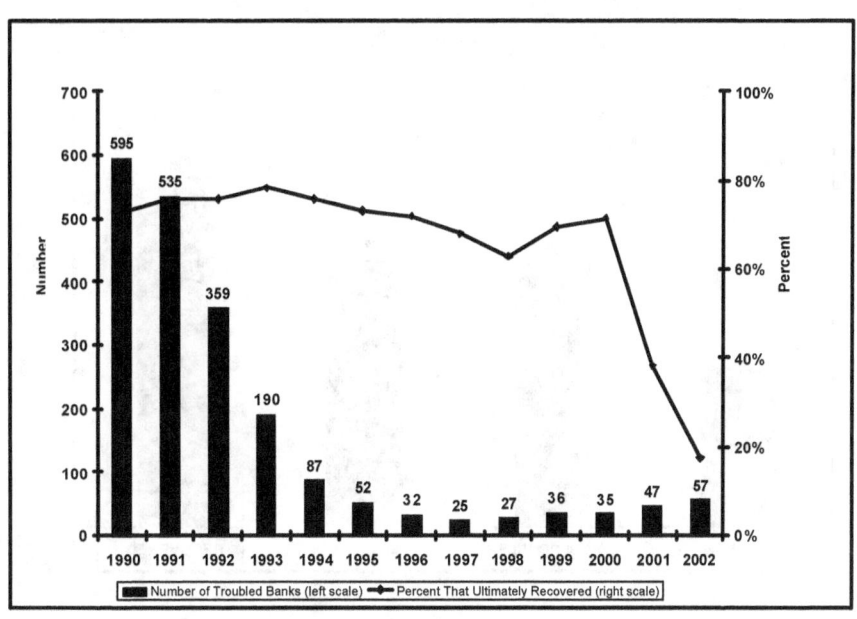

Figure 4
External and Internal Capital Injections
in Troubled Banks That Recovered
(12 months before recovery)

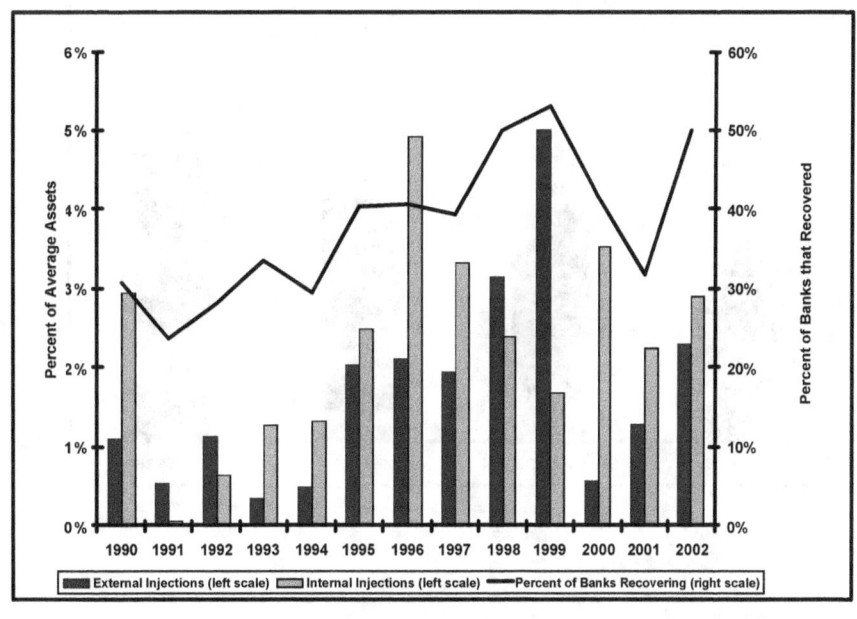

Figure 5
Increases in Net Interest Income

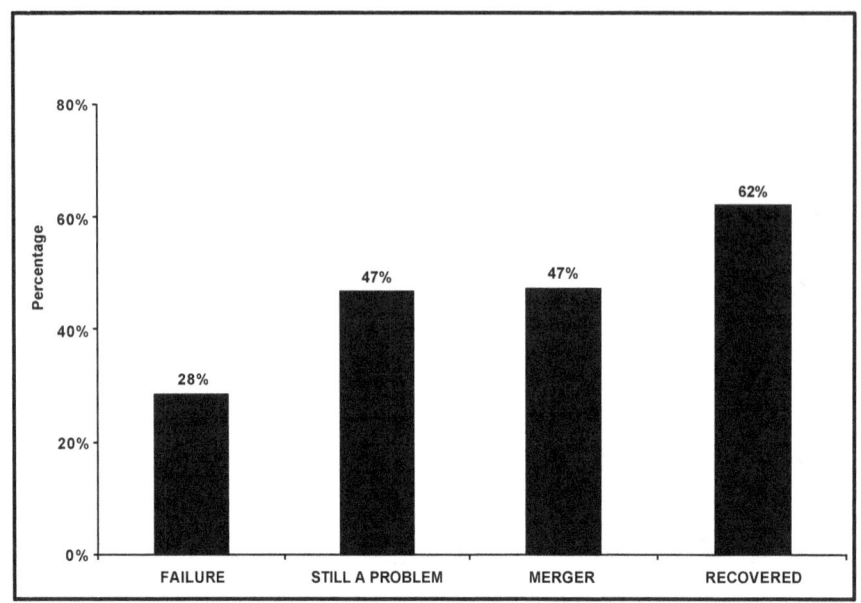

Figure 6
Increases in Net Noninterest Income

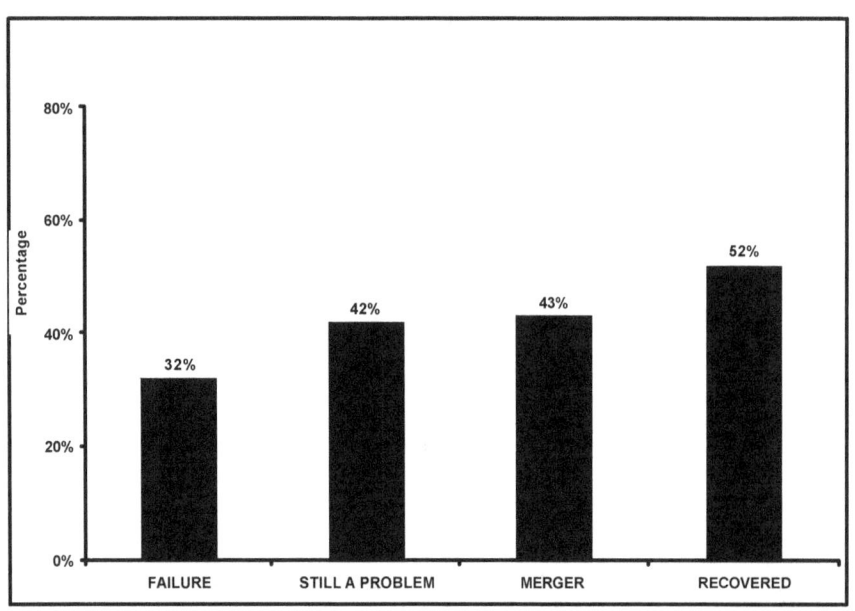

28

Figure 7
Increases in Loss Provision

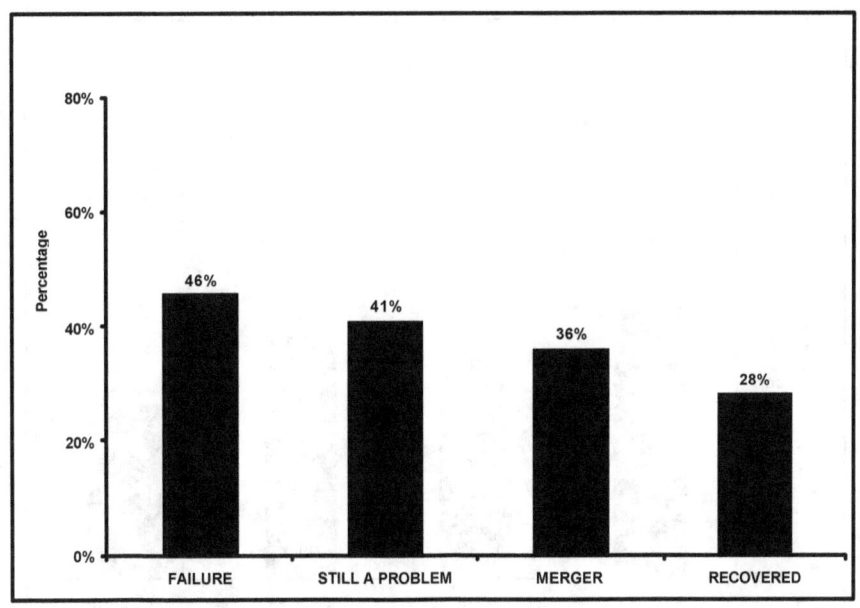

Figure 8
Increases in Loan-Loss Reserves

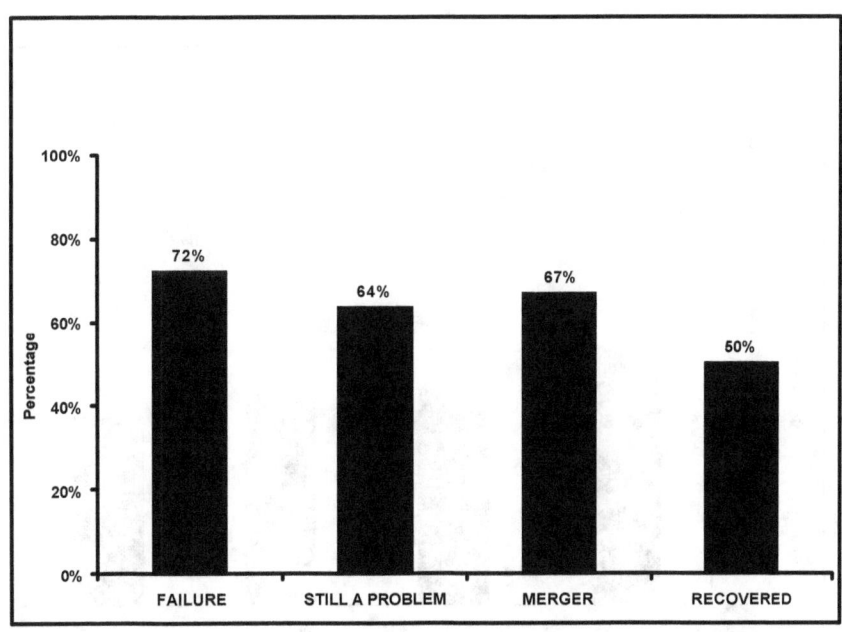

Figure 9
Increases in 30–89 Days Past-Due Loans

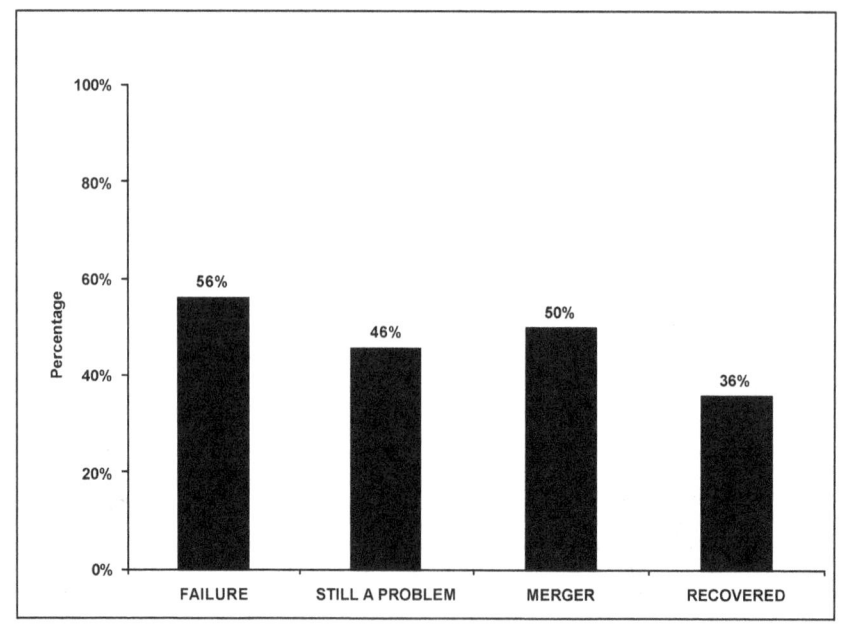

Figure 10
Increases in Past-Due Loans 90 Days or More

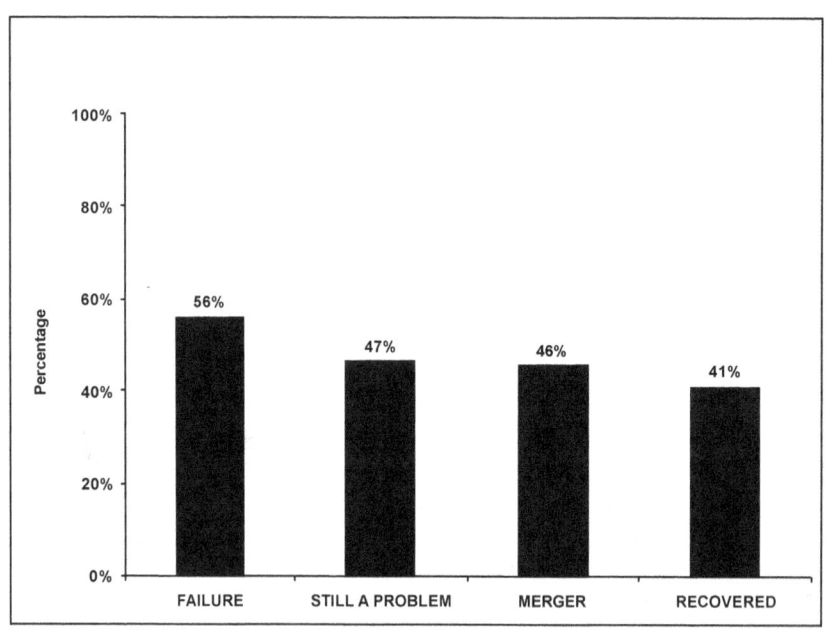

Figure 11
Increases in Nonaccrual Loan

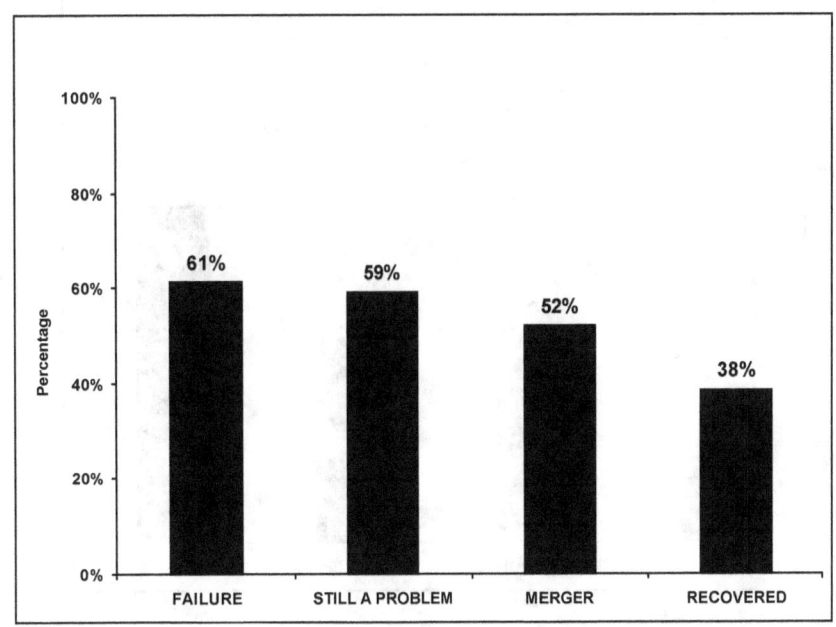

Figure 12
Increases in Other Real Estate Owned

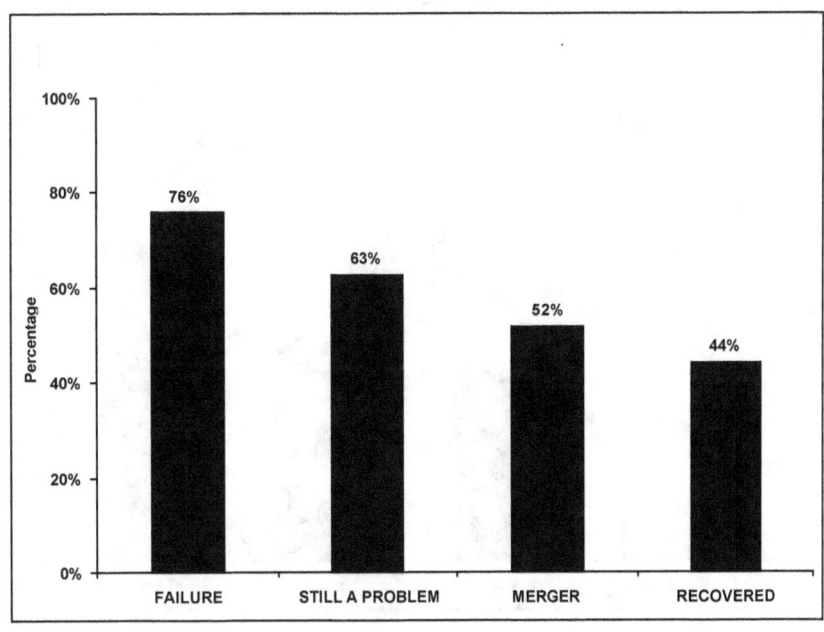

Figure 13
Increases in Risk-Based Capital

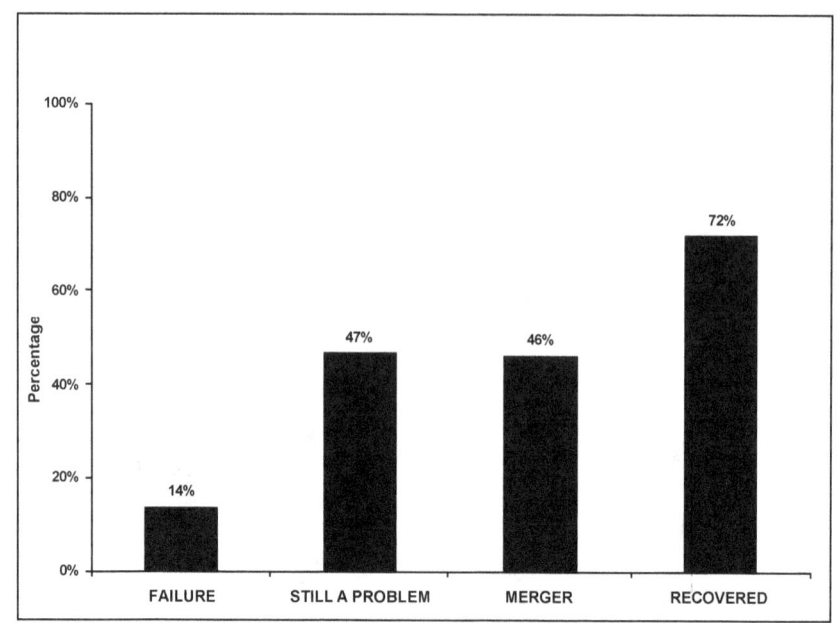

Figure 14
Increases in Tangible Capital

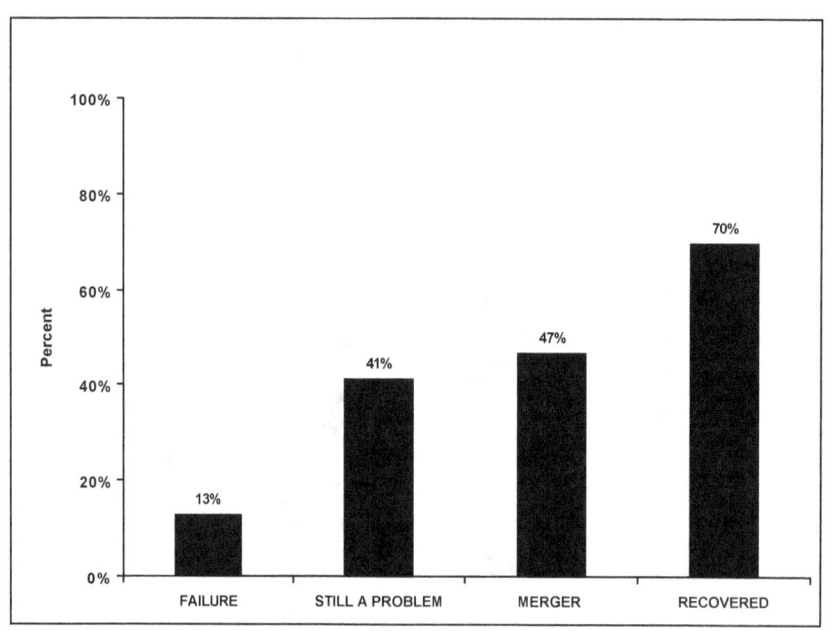

Figure 15
Increases in Volatile Liabilities

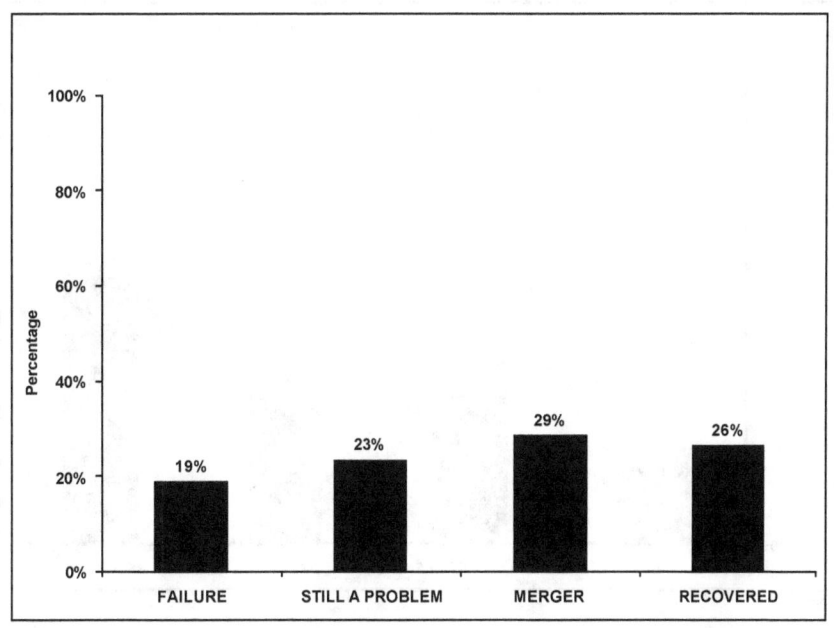

Figure 16
Increases in Loans and Securities with Maturities
Greater than or Equal to Five Years

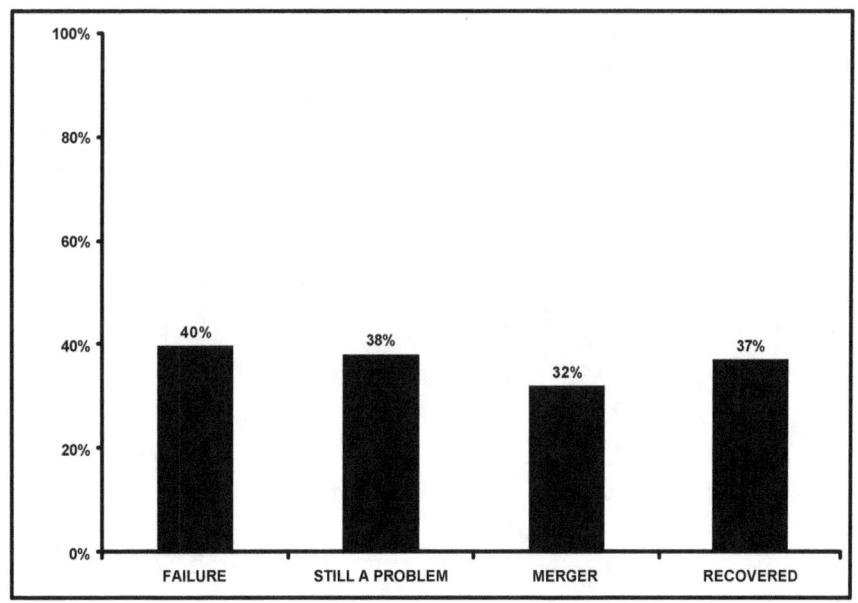

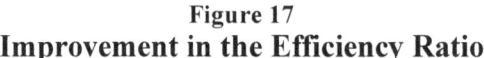

Figure 17
Improvement in the Efficiency Ratio

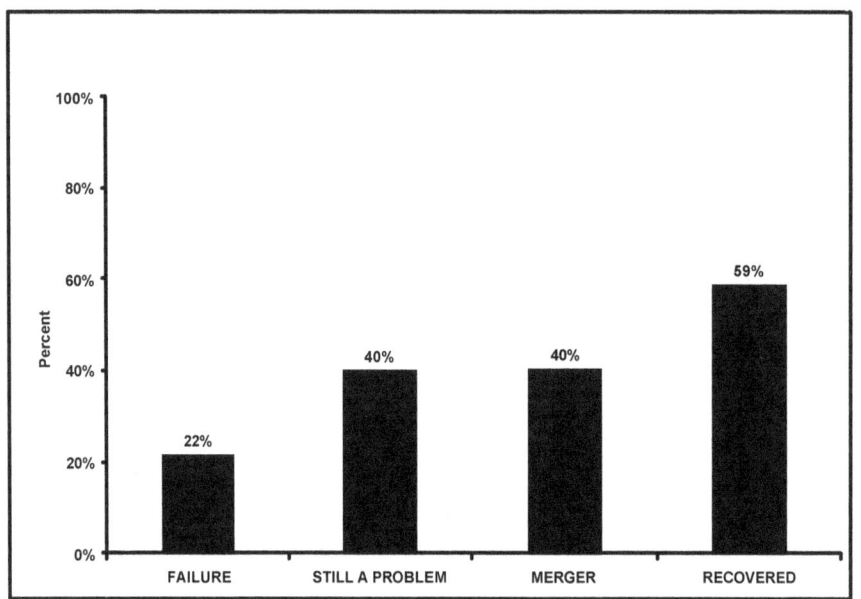

34

Figure 18
Recovered
(One-Year-Ahead Forecasts versus Actual)

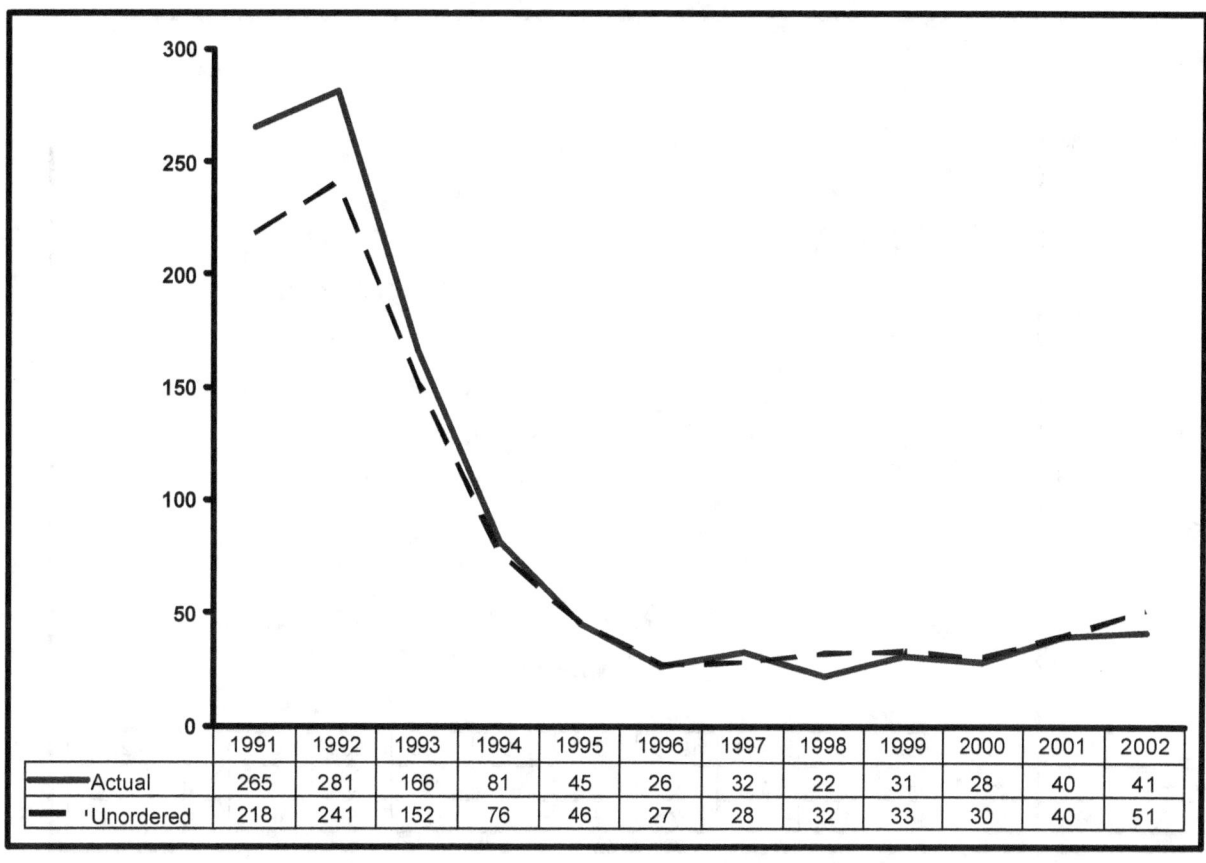

	1991	1992	1993	1994	1995	1996	1997	1998	1999	2000	2001	2002
Actual	265	281	166	81	45	26	32	22	31	28	40	41
Unordered	218	241	152	76	46	27	28	32	33	30	40	51

35

Figure 19
Acquired
(One-Year-Ahead Forecasts versus Actual)

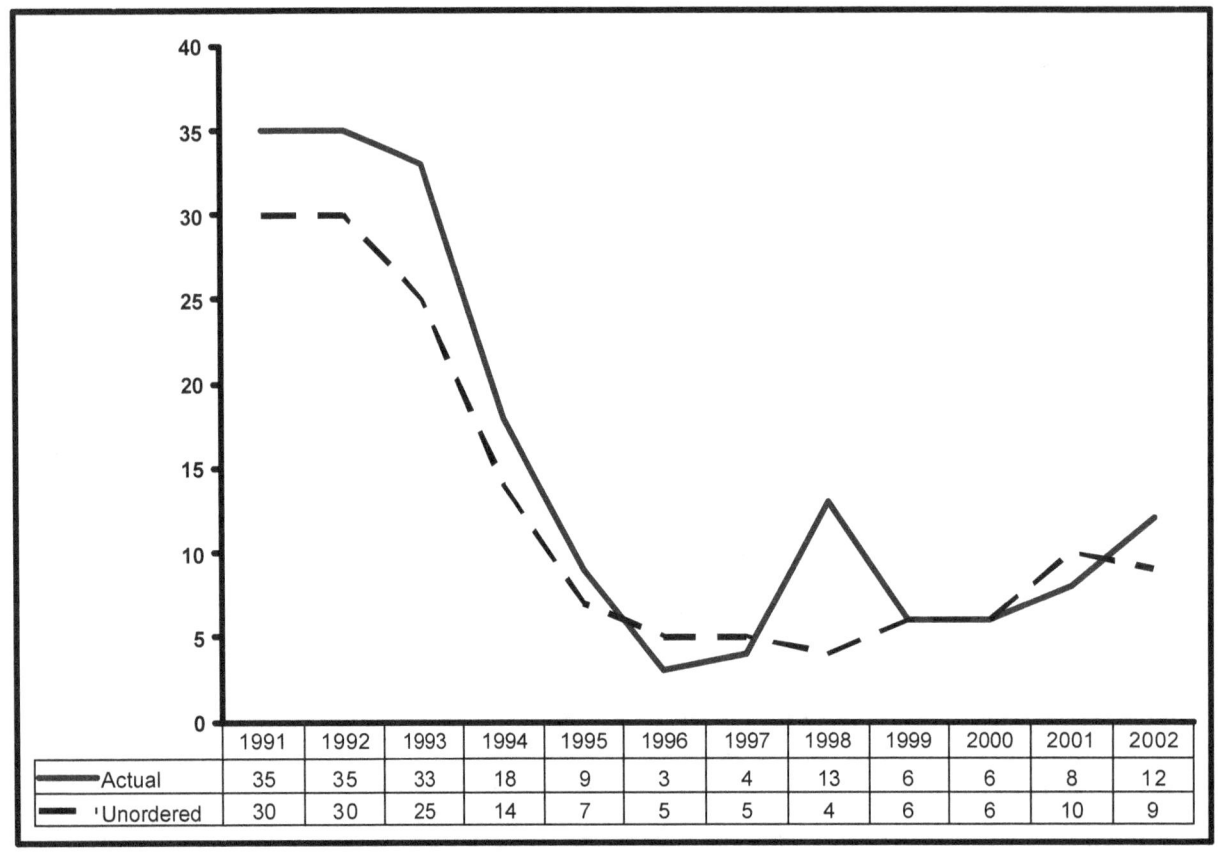

	1991	1992	1993	1994	1995	1996	1997	1998	1999	2000	2001	2002
Actual	35	35	33	18	9	3	4	13	6	6	8	12
'Unordered	30	30	25	14	7	5	5	4	6	6	10	9

Figure 20
Continued as a Problem
(One-Year-Ahead Forecasts versus Actual)

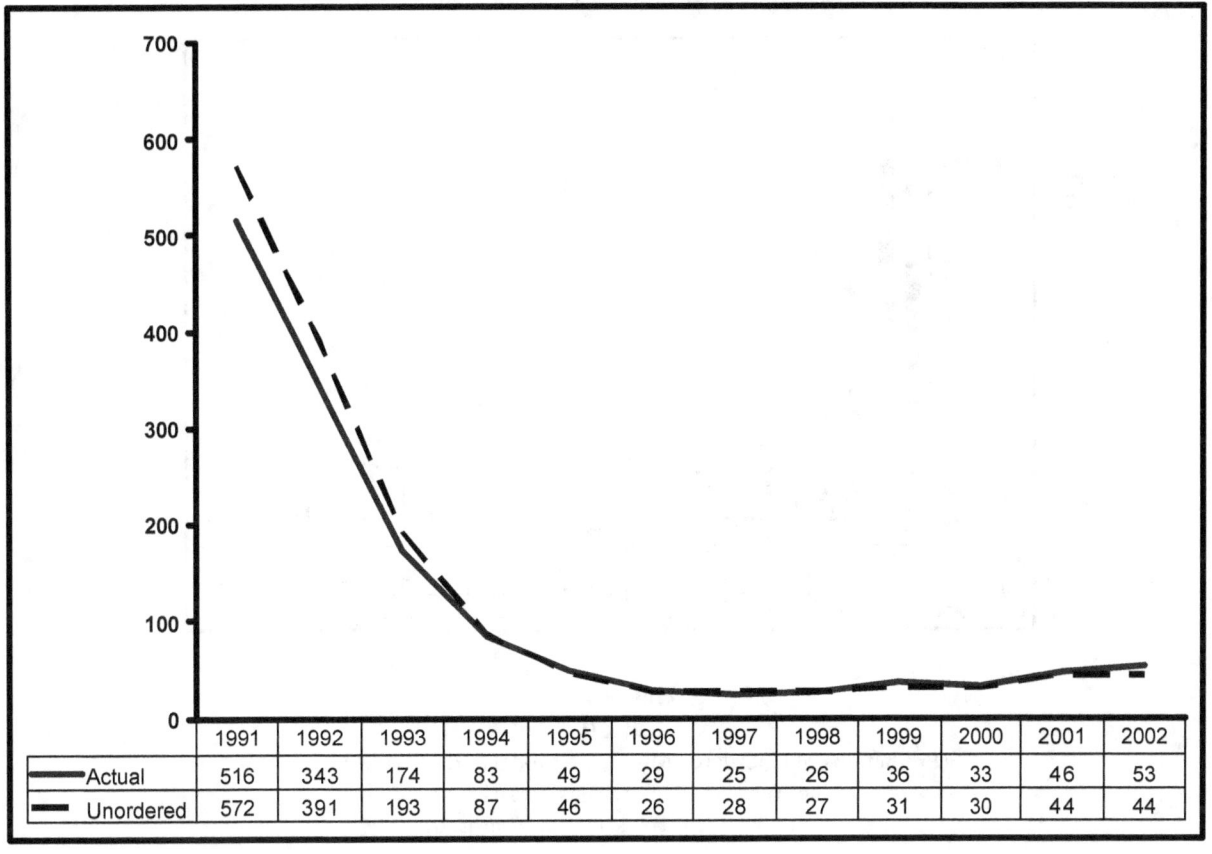

	1991	1992	1993	1994	1995	1996	1997	1998	1999	2000	2001	2002
Actual	516	343	174	83	49	29	25	26	36	33	46	53
Unordered	572	391	193	87	46	26	28	27	31	30	44	44

Figure 21
Failed
(Predictions of Unordered Multistate and Bivariate Models
One-Year-Ahead Forecasts versus Actual)

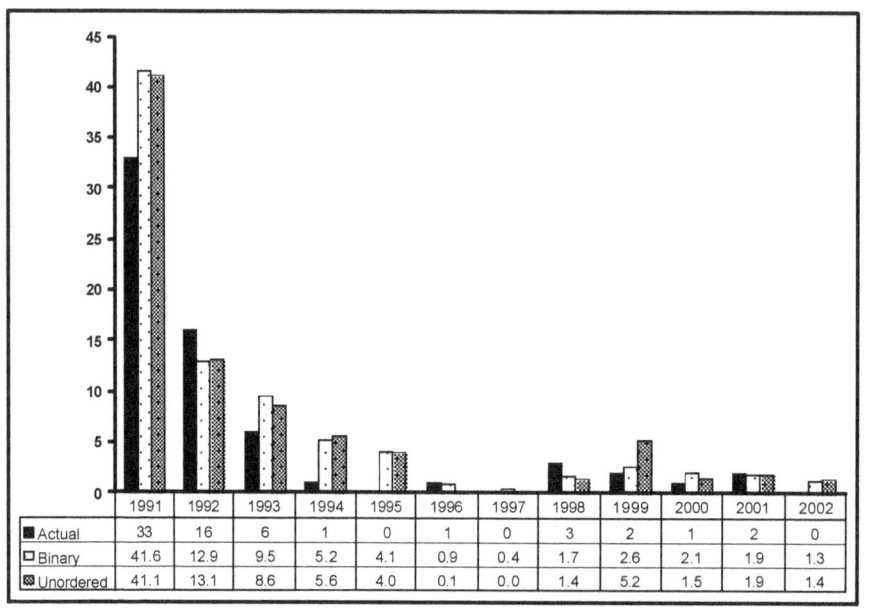

	1991	1992	1993	1994	1995	1996	1997	1998	1999	2000	2001	2002
■ Actual	33	16	6	1	0	1	0	3	2	1	2	0
□ Binary	41.6	12.9	9.5	5.2	4.1	0.9	0.4	1.7	2.6	2.1	1.9	1.3
▓ Unordered	41.1	13.1	8.6	5.6	4.0	0.1	0.0	1.4	5.2	1.5	1.9	1.4

Figure 22
Failed
(Predictions of Unordered Multistate Model and LDM Models
One-Year-Ahead Forecasts versus Actual
Total Problem-Bank List at Year-End)

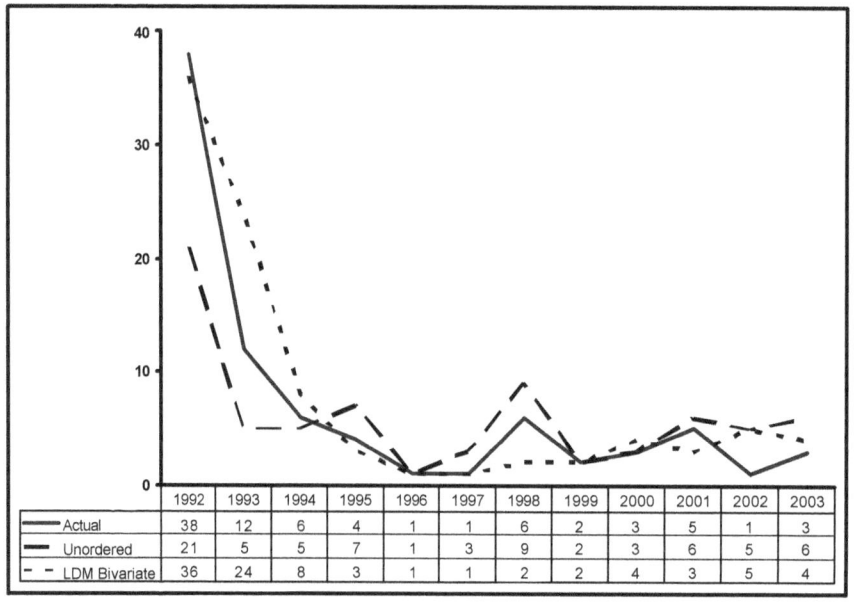

	1992	1993	1994	1995	1996	1997	1998	1999	2000	2001	2002	2003
Actual	38	12	6	4	1	1	6	2	3	5	1	3
Unordered	21	5	5	7	1	3	9	2	3	6	5	6
LDM Bivariate	36	24	8	3	1	1	2	2	4	3	5	4

38

Table 1
Explanatory Variables and Expected Signs for Predicting Nonfailure versus Failure States

Variable	Sign
Capital	
Tangible Equity Capital	+
Capital Injections:	
From BHC	+
Outside	+
Asset Quality	
Past-Due Loans (30 - 89 days)	-
Past-Due Loans (90+ days)	-
Nonaccrual Loans and Leases	-
Other Real Estate Owned	-
Allowance for Loan Loss	+
Management	
Efficiency Ratio	-
Earnings	
Total Interest Income	+
Total Noninterest income	+
Total Interest Expense	-
Loan-Loss Provision	-
Loan Charge-offs	-
Expenses on Premises	-
Salaries	-
Other noninterest expense	-
Liquidity	
Volatile Liabilities	-
Loans + Securities > Five Years	+

Table 2
Mean and Standard Errors for Financial Variables, by State
(Standard Errors in Parentheses)

Variable	Recover	Merge	Remain a Problem	Fail
Number of Banks	1,326	228	2,077	116
Capital				
Tangible Equity Capital	6.68 ***	6.57 ***	6.39 ***	3.90 ***
	(0.08)	(0.20)	(0.07)	(0.29)
Capital Injections:				
From BHC	0.19 ***	0.41 ***	0.20 ***	0.14 *
	(0.02)	(0.06)	(0.02)	(0.08)
Outside	0.36 ***	0.29 ***	0.29 ***	0.42 ***
	(0.04)	(0.09)	(0.03)	(0.13)
Asset Quality				
Past-Due Loans (30 - 89 days)	1.88 ***	2.12 ***	2.43 ***	3.08 ***
	(0.04)	(0.10)	(0.03)	(0.14)
Past-Due Loans (90+ days)	0.59 ***	0.65 ***	0.92 ***	1.17 ***
	(0.04)	(0.09)	(0.03)	(0.13)
Nonaccrual Loans and Leases	2.17 ***	2.56 ***	2.64 ***	3.82 ***
	(0.06)	(0.14)	(0.05)	(0.20)
Other Real Estate Owned	2.00 ***	1.88 ***	2.60 ***	3.19
	(0.07)	(0.17)	(0.06)	(0.23) ***
Allowance for Loan Loss	1.69 ***	1.97 ***	1.72 ***	2.11 ***
	(0.03)	(0.07)	(0.02)	(0.10)
Management				
Efficiency Ratio	88.32 ***	94.15 ***	94.43 ***	115.77 ***
	(0.67)	(1.62)	(0.54)	(2.28)

Significance at 1%, 5% and 10% levels are indicated by ***, **, and * asterisks, respectively.

Table 2 (Continued)
Mean and Standard Errors for Financial Variables, by State
(Standard Errors in Parentheses)

Variable	Recover	Merge	Remain a Problem	Fail
Number of Banks	1,326	228	2,077	116
Earnings				
Total Interest Income	8.80 ***	8.99 ***	9.59 ***	10.58 ***
	(0.09)	(0.21)	(0.07)	(0.29)
Total Noninterest income	1.41 ***	1.44 ***	1.45 ***	1.98 ***
	(0.06)	(0.15)	(0.05)	(0.21)
Total Interest Expense	4.47 ***	4.51 ***	5.27 ***	6.51 ***
	(0.06)	(0.14)	(0.05)	(0.20)
Loan-Loss Provision	1.35 ***	2.23 ***	1.81 ***	3.21 ***
	(0.07)	(0.16)	(0.05)	(0.22)
Loan Charge-offs	1.46 ***	1.78 ***	1.80 ***	2.86 ***
	(0.05)	(0.12)	(0.04)	(0.17)
Expenses on Premises	0.68 ***	0.75 ***	0.77 ***	0.96 ***
	(0.01)	(0.03)	(0.01)	(0.04)
Salaries	2.06 ***	2.08 ***	2.18 ***	2.56 ***
	(0.03)	(0.08)	(0.03)	(0.11)
Other noninterest expense	2.23 ***	2.54 ***	2.43 ***	3.29 ***
	(0.05)	(0.11)	(0.04)	(0.16)
Liquidity				
Volatile Liabilities	13.26 ***	13.62 ***	14.96 ***	15.04 ***
	(0.27)	(0.65)	(0.22)	(0.91)
Loans + Securities > Five Years	66.13 ***	68.11 ***	68.71 ***	68.04 ***
	(0.31)	(0.76)	(0.25)	(1.06)

Significance at 1%, 5% and 10% levels are indicated by ***, **, and * asterisks, respectively.

Table 3
Differences in Means and Standard Errors
of Financial Variables for Selected Pairs
(Standard Errors in Parentheses)

Variable	Recover - Merge	Recover - Remain a Problem	Recover - Fail	Merge - Remain a Problem	Remain a Problem - Fail	Merge - Fail
Capital						
Tangible Equity Capital	0.10	0.29 **	2.78 ***	0.19	2.49 ***	2.68 ***
	(0.22)	(0.11)	(0.30)	(0.22)	(0.29)	(0.35)
Capital Injections:						
From BHC	-0.22 ***	(0.01)	0.04	0.21 ***	0.05	0.26 **
	(0.06)	(0.03)	(0.08)	(0.06)	(0.08)	(0.10)
Outside	0.07	0.08	(0.06)	0.00	-0.14	-0.13
	(0.10)	(0.05)	(0.13)	(0.10)	(0.13)	(0.16)
Asset Quality						
Past-Due Loans (30 - 89 days)	-0.24 **	-0.55 ***	-1.20 ***	-0.31 **	-0.65 ***	-0.96 ***
	(0.11)	(0.05)	(0.15)	(0.11)	(0.15)	(0.18)
Past-Due Loans (90+ days)	-0.06	-0.33 ***	-0.58 ***	-0.27 **	-0.25 *	-0.52 ***
	(0.10)	(0.05)	(0.13)	(0.10)	(0.13)	(0.16)
Nonaccrual Loans and Leases	-0.39 **	-0.47 ***	-1.65 ***	-0.09	-1.18 ***	-1.27 ***
	(0.15)	(0.07)	(0.20)	(0.15)	(0.20)	(0.24)
Other Real Estate Owned	0.12	-0.59 ***	-1.19 ***	-0.72 ***	-0.59 **	-1.31 ***
	(0.18)	(0.09)	(0.24)	(0.18)	(0.24)	(0.29)
Allowance for Loan Loss	-0.29 ***	-0.04	-0.42 ***	0.25 **	-0.38 ***	-0.13
	(0.08)	(0.04)	(0.11)	(0.08)	(0.11)	(0.13)
Management						
Efficiency Ratio	-5.83 ***	-6.10 ***	-27.44 ***	-0.28	-21.34 ***	-21.62 ***
	(1.76)	(0.86)	(2.37)	(1.71)	(2.34)	(2.79)

Significance at 1%, 5% and 10% levels are indicated by ***, **, and * asterisks, respectively.

Table 3 (Continued)
Differences in Means and Standard Errors
of Financial Variables for Selected Pairs
(Standard Errors in Parentheses)

Variable	Recover - Merge	Recover - Remain a Problem	Recover - Fail	Merge - Remain a Problem	Remain a Problem - Fail	Merge - Fail
Earnings						
Total Interest Income	-0.19	-0.79 ***	-1.78 ***	-0.60 **	-0.99 ***	-1.59 ***
	(0.22)	(0.11)	(0.30)	(0.22)	(0.30)	(0.36)
Total Noninterest income	-0.03	-0.04	-0.57 **	-0.01	-0.53 **	-0.54 **
	(0.17)	(0.08)	(0.22)	(0.16)	(0.22)	(0.26)
Total Interest Expense	-0.03	-0.79 ***	-2.03 ***	-0.76 ***	-1.24 ***	-2.00 ***
	(0.15)	(0.07)	(0.21)	(0.15)	(0.20)	(0.24)
Loan-Loss Provision	-0.88 ***	-0.46 ***	-1.85 ***	0.42 **	-1.40 ***	-0.97 ***
	(0.17)	(0.08)	(0.23)	(0.17)	(0.23)	(0.27)
Loan Charge-offs	-0.32 **	-0.33 ***	-1.39 ***	-0.02	-1.06 ***	-1.08 ***
	(0.13)	(0.07)	(0.18)	(0.13)	(0.18)	(0.21)
Expenses on Premises	-0.07 **	-0.09 ***	-0.28 ***	-0.02	-0.19 ***	-0.21 ***
	(0.03)	(0.02)	(0.04)	(0.03)	(0.04)	(0.05)
Salaries	-0.03	-0.12 **	-0.50 ***	-0.09	-0.38 ***	-0.48 ***
	(0.08)	(0.04)	(0.11)	(0.08)	(0.11)	(0.13)
Other non-int. exp	-0.30 **	-0.20 ***	-1.06 ***	0.11	-0.86 ***	-0.76 ***
	(0.12)	(0.06)	(0.16)	(0.12)	(0.16)	(0.19)
Liquidity						
Volatile Liabilities	-0.36	-1.70 ***	-1.78 *	-1.34 *	-0.09	-1.43
	(0.70)	(0.35)	(0.95)	(0.69)	(0.94)	(1.12)
Loans + Securities > Five Years	-1.98 **	-2.57 ***	-1.91 *	-0.60	0.66	0.07
	(0.82)	(0.40)	(1.11)	(0.80)	(1.09)	(1.31)

Significance at 1%, 5% and 10% levels are indicated by ***, **, and * asterisks, respectively.

Table 4
Selected Descriptive Statistics for Data in Logits: Mean, Standard Deviation, and Minimum and Maximum Values of Financial Ratios for Each State

Variable	All	Recover	Merge	Remain a Problem	Fail
Number of Banks	3,747	1,326	228	2,077	116
Capital					
Tangible Equity Capital					
Mean	6.42	6.68	6.57	6.39	3.90
Standard Deviation	3.12	2.54	3.42	3.37	2.76
Minimum	-4.77	-0.10	-4.77	-1.26	-1.37
Maximum	63.10	38.34	34.52	63.10	15.79
Capital Injections:					
From BHC					
Mean	0.20	0.19	0.41	0.20	0.14
Standard Deviation	0.87	0.82	1.41	0.84	0.65
Minimum	-1.07	-1.07	0.00	-0.93	-0.02
Maximum	12.87	9.98	12.87	8.97	4.74
Outside					
Mean	0.36	0.36	0.29	0.29	0.42
Standard Deviation	1.38	1.46	1.52	1.25	2.24
Minimum	-2.03	-1.89	-0.07	-2.03	-0.62
Maximum	25.16	15.98	15.98	25.16	18.38
Asset Quality					
Past-Due Loans (30 - 89 days)					
Mean	2.24	1.88	2.12	2.43	3.08
Standard Deviation	1.58	1.38	1.84	1.60	1.95
Minimum	0.00	0.00	0.00	0.00	0.25
Maximum	18.66	12.41	18.66	13.96	9.59
Past-Due Loans (90+ days)					
Mean	0.79	0.59	0.65	0.92	1.17
Standard Deviation	1.39	0.81	0.81	1.66	1.82
Minimum	0.00	0.00	0.00	0.00	0.00
Maximum	44.66	10.25	6.22	44.66	14.42
Nonaccrual Loans and Leases					
Mean	2.51	2.17	2.56	2.64	3.82
Standard Deviation	2.13	1.83	2.62	2.19	2.36
Minimum	0.00	0.00	0.00	0.00	0.05
Maximum	24.71	15.60	24.71	17.67	11.18
Other Real Estate Owned					
Mean	2.36	2.00	1.88	2.60	3.19
Standard Deviation	2.55	2.13	1.97	2.79	2.63
Minimum	-10.05	0.00	0.00	-10.05	-0.24
Maximum	20.20	18.61	10.99	20.20	12.48
Allowance for Loan Loss					
Mean	1.74	1.69	1.97	1.72	2.11
Standard Deviation	1.13	1.08	2.01	1.03	0.95
Minimum	0.11	0.11	0.36	0.14	0.28
Maximum	26.45	19.82	26.45	14.13	5.63
Management					
Efficiency Ratio					
Mean	92.91	88.32	94.15	94.43	115.77
Standard Deviation	25.00	22.85	25.34	25.09	29.99
Minimum	-30.64	-30.64	35.09	29.38	26.72
Maximum	198.71	193.89	195.03	198.71	194.40

Table 4 (Continued)
Selected Descriptive Statistics for Data in Logits: Mean, Standard Deviation, and Minimum andMaximum Values of Financial Ratios for Each State

Variable	All	Recover	Merge	Remain a Problem	Fail
Earnings					
Total Interest Income					
Mean	9.30	8.80	8.99	9.59	10.58
Standard Deviation	3.14	2.60	4.63	3.14	4.11
Minimum	-0.01	-0.01	5.24	0.97	4.47
Maximum	64.32	33.69	64.32	32.78	26.25
Total Noninterest income					
Mean	1.45	1.41	1.44	1.45	1.98
Standard Deviation	2.31	2.18	1.84	2.38	3.20
Minimum	-0.09	-0.09	0.00	-0.05	0.18
Maximum	46.35	37.82	16.34	46.35	30.51
Total Interest Expense					
Mean	4.98	4.47	4.51	5.27	6.51
Standard Deviation	2.18	1.76	2.25	2.28	2.95
Minimum	-0.68	-0.68	1.25	0.25	0.95
Maximum	17.01	14.74	15.42	17.01	16.57
Loan-Loss Provision					
Mean	1.72	1.35	2.23	1.81	3.21
Standard Deviation	2.43	1.72	6.07	2.02	2.69
Minimum	-13.56	-2.17	-1.54	-13.56	-0.42
Maximum	87.33	23.14	87.33	24.55	13.82
Loan Charge-offs					
Mean	1.71	1.46	1.78	1.80	2.86
Standard Deviation	1.89	1.41	3.52	1.86	2.06
Minimum	-6.32	-0.49	-6.32	0.00	0.25
Maximum	47.20	19.12	47.20	24.12	11.50
Expenses on Premises					
Mean	0.75	0.68	0.75	0.77	0.96
Standard Deviation	0.46	0.40	0.44	0.47	0.67
Minimum	-0.48	-0.48	0.00	-0.04	0.15
Maximum	4.46	3.38	2.79	4.35	4.46
Salaries					
Mean	2.14	2.06	2.08	2.18	2.56
Standard Deviation	1.18	0.95	0.99	1.23	2.32
Minimum	0.00	0.06	0.00	0.04	0.43
Maximum	22.99	16.14	9.17	22.36	22.99
Other noninterest expense					
Mean	2.39	2.23	2.54	2.43	3.29
Standard Deviation	1.68	1.55	2.43	1.61	2.12
Minimum	-3.03	-3.03	0.45	-0.41	0.71
Maximum	32.70	22.46	32.70	25.38	14.86
Liquidity					
Volatile Liabilities					
Mean	14.28	13.26	13.62	14.96	15.04
Standard Deviation	9.85	9.51	11.08	9.90	9.26
Minimum	0.00	0.00	0.00	0.00	0.00
Maximum	90.19	86.08	90.19	89.43	51.54
Loans + Securities > Five years					
Mean	67.74	66.13	68.11	68.71	68.04
Standard Deviation	11.51	11.39	12.15	11.43	11.21
Minimum	19.40	24.31	19.40	22.14	37.34
Maximum	102.02	102.02	96.38	101.05	90.33

Table 5
Multinomial Logit Regressions of Determinants of Bank State: Recovery versus Failure
Estimation Period (Years)

Explanatory Variables	1990	1991	1992	1993	1993-94	1993-95	1993-96	1993-97	1994-98	1995-99	1996-00	1997-01	1998-02
Intercept													
Constant	-0.2388	10.6388 ***	-2.0548	-2.8325	8.4024 *	7.0800 *	6.2905	6.0942	14.2305	-2.8352	3.9788	1.0819	-0.6638
Capital													
Tangible Equity for PCA	0.7743 ***	1.0350 ***	0.7071 ***	-0.1248	-0.1827	-0.0345	-0.0198	-0.0262	1.4338	0.2043	-0.0802	-0.0156	-0.0120
BHC Capital Injections	2.0621	-0.3816	0.6065	0.5490	0.4402	0.3137	0.3806	0.3978	-3.1364	-0.6126	-0.3481	-0.6839 *	-0.6238 *
External Capital Injections	0.0021	0.1636	5.1764 **	0.8219	1.1397	1.5649	1.5940	1.6146	-0.9101	-0.3444 *	-0.2561	-0.2861 **	-0.2477
Asset Quality													
Loans Past Due 30 to 89 Days	-0.4142 ***	-0.4417 ***	-0.2429	-0.8305 **	-0.4773 **	-0.2567	-0.1913	-0.1730	0.5548	0.3001	0.5276	0.1184	0.0400
Loans Past Due 90 Days or More	-0.4630 ***	-0.1805	-0.5600	-0.3232	-0.1968	-0.3677 **	-0.4260 ***	-0.4530 ***	-1.0422 **	-0.5484 ***	-0.3320	-0.1901	0.0021
Nonaccrual Loans and Leases	-0.2163 **	-0.3689 ***	-0.4007 **	-0.7762 *	-0.6210 ***	-0.5803 ***	-0.6002 ***	-0.6283 ***	-2.9354 **	-0.6012 **	-0.3506	-0.2224	-0.1628
Other Real Estate Owned	-0.3847 ***	-0.2984 ***	0.1820	0.3759	0.3007	0.2900	0.3299	0.3245	7.6096 **	0.6112	0.0660	-0.0690	-0.1354
Allowance for Loan Losses	0.3333	0.7585 ***	0.1987	2.5538 **	0.9456 *	0.7284	0.7687 *	0.7911 *	4.1672	0.8971	1.0031	1.0392	0.9083
Management													
Efficiency Ratio	-0.0010	-0.0218	-0.0233	0.0277	-0.0398	-0.0406	-0.0328	-0.0341	-0.0417	0.0685	0.0308	0.0411	0.0498
Earnings													
Total Interest Income	1.0295	-0.9335	0.6710	2.3293	-0.3460	-0.3550	-0.1461	-0.1235	-3.0691	0.4429	0.4718	0.6600	1.0897
Total Noninterest Income	0.6360	-0.6387	0.3575	2.2171 *	0.4048	0.1514	0.2814	0.2917	-2.3035	0.7560	0.4635	0.5670	0.7607
Total Interest Expense	-1.2585 *	-0.0224	-0.6493	-1.2851	0.7541	0.3780	0.0680	0.0577	-0.7468	-0.9387	-1.0633	-1.3890 *	-1.6172
Loan-loss Provision	-0.7479 ***	-0.6765 ***	-0.1868	-1.2186 *	-0.9301 **	-0.8185 **	-0.9011 **	-0.9159 **	0.1979	-0.5587	-0.8741	-0.6199	-0.3175
Loan Chargeoffs	0.7248 ***	0.6950 ***	-0.4833	0.8751	0.6614	0.7422	0.7013 *	0.6955 **	1.5349	0.6323	0.6174	0.4337	0.2000
Expenses on Premises	-0.3109	-0.3120	-2.5638	-1.7553	-0.6163	-0.9336	-1.0243	-0.9938	-2.3193	-2.3415	-2.7488 *	-3.4456 **	-3.7522 **
Salaries	-1.4292 **	0.5001	0.9138	-1.6762	-0.0150	0.1143	-0.0836	-0.1369	7.9328	-0.6335	-0.3216	-0.3277	-0.2640
Other Noninterest Expense	-0.3044	0.0733	-0.4493	-3.4496 **	-0.7108	-0.3225	-0.4617	-0.4250	-0.0248	-1.1180	-0.7435 *	-0.7250	-1.2015
Liquidity													
Volatile Liabilities	-0.0130	0.0180	0.0191	-0.0726	-0.0456	-0.0072	0.0087	0.0117	-0.3340 *	-0.0723 *	-0.0434	-0.0387	-0.0349
Loans Plus Securities >= Five years	0.0025	0.0033	0.0730	0.0743	0.0807	0.0792	0.0798	0.0856	0.0863	0.0708	0.0208	0.0473	0.0345
Log Likelihood	-584.9	-662.5	-561.8	-328.8	-505.8	-597.7	-660.9	-708.4	-416.7	-339.3	-315.9	-348.5	-410.6
Number of Observations	866	897	713	413	607	717	781	843	495	377	341	375	428
Akaike Information Criteria	1289.8	1445.0	1243.6	777.6	1131.6	1315.4	1441.8	1536.8	953.4	798.5	751.7	816.9	941.3
Pseudo R squared	0.090	0.222	0.170	0.195	0.162	0.159	0.144	0.145	0.172	0.121	0.102	0.103	0.078

Significance at 1%, 5% and 10% levels are indicated by ***, **, and * asterisks, respectively.

46

Table 6
Multinomial Logit Regressions of Determinants of Bank State: Merger versus Failure
Estimation Period (Years)

Explanatory Variables	1990	1991	1992	1993	1993-94	1993-95	1993-96	1993-97	1994-98	1995-99	1996-00	1997-01	1998-02
Intercept													
Constant	-4.4684	9.6836 **	-7.5929	-5.191	4.203	4.6942	4.5547	4.7692	11.3291	-5.1144	0.9346	-0.6199	-1.9189
Capital													
Tangible Equity for PCA	0.5301 **	0.8500 ***	0.7454 ***	-0.0461	-0.1382	-0.0093	-0.0002	-0.0191	1.4089	0.2249	-0.0238	-0.0080	-0.0014
BHC Capital Injections	2.1647	-0.1048	0.3075	1.0384	0.7004	0.5830	0.5993	0.5579	-3.1430	-0.8561	-0.5000	-0.7831 *	-0.5443
External Capital Injections	-0.9151	-0.0810	5.0893 **	0.8027	0.9729	1.3522	1.3519	1.3907	-1.6622 **	-1.2036 **	-0.5297 *	-0.4764 *	-0.4560 *
Asset Quality													
Loans Past Due 30 to 89 Days	-0.6823 **	-0.4077 **	-0.2239	-0.8464 **	-0.4781 **	-0.1863	-0.2035	-0.1915	0.6182	0.3477	0.5696	0.2731	0.2128
Loans Past Due 90 Days or More	-0.3236	-0.0706	-0.5440	-0.1931	-0.2134	-0.5354 **	-0.5049 **	-0.5198 **	-0.9865 **	-0.3893 *	-0.2086	-0.1001	0.0566
Nonaccrual Loans and Leases	-0.2397	-0.4158 ***	-0.3294 **	-0.7045	-0.6407 ***	-0.5988 ***	-0.6019 ***	-0.6018 ***	-2.9516 **	-0.4764 *	-0.1760	-0.0955	-0.1115
Other Real Estate Owned	-0.1902 *	-0.4054 ***	0.2594	0.3367	0.3322	0.2715	0.3054	0.3055	7.6746 **	0.5882	0.0078	-0.0945	-0.1525
Allowance for Loan Losses	0.3356	0.8715 ***	0.3666	2.6342 **	1.2752 **	0.9467 **	0.9844 **	0.9958 *	4.3713	0.5819	0.7722	0.8808	0.8598
Management													
Efficiency Ratio	0.0094	-0.0345	-0.0171	0.0437	-0.0179	-0.0297	-0.0320	-0.0379	-0.0522	0.0580	0.0218	0.0396	0.0435
Earnings													
Total Interest Income	1.1992	-1.5633 **	0.5040	2.2421	-0.1898	-0.5105	-0.3677	-0.3640	-3.3443	0.2597	0.5499	0.6946	0.9715
Total Noninterest Income	0.7799	-1.4107 **	0.2819	2.5038 **	0.5521	0.1408	0.1259	0.0759	-2.6277	0.6042	0.4134	0.6291	0.6470
Total Interest Expense	-0.9474	0.7870	-0.4657	-0.8863	0.7604	0.6581	0.4352	0.4075	-0.3228	-0.5881	-0.7982	-1.1075	-1.3550
Loan-loss Provision	0.1164	-0.1086	0.0177 ***	-1.0359	-0.6691	-0.5882	-0.6731 **	-0.7569 **	0.2790	-0.6447	-0.7495	-0.5020	-0.2115
Loan Chargeoffs	-0.0145	0.0398	-0.7365 ***	0.8755	0.3109	0.3865	0.3321	0.3975	1.0550	0.7349	0.5245	0.3932	0.1833
Expenses on Premises	-0.8320	1.1644	-1.5325	-1.7446	-0.2103	-0.4991	-0.4863	-0.3517	-1.2111	-1.3686	-1.4539	-2.0358	-2.7002
Salaries	-1.7712 *	1.4012 *	0.8435	-1.5131	-0.0220	0.2606	0.1441	0.1638	8.1622	-0.6658	-0.5979	-0.7600	-0.4629
Other Noninterest Expense	-0.2371 *	0.6104 **	-0.0030 **	-4.1409	-1.3090	-0.4806	-0.4177	-0.3441	0.2520	-0.8389	-0.6434	-0.8411	-1.0175
Liquidity													
Volatile Liabilities	-0.0085	-0.0177	0.0025	-0.1507 *	-0.1159	-0.0679	-0.0431	-0.0379	-0.3553 **	-0.0813 *	-0.0253	-0.0431	-0.0287
Loans Plus Securities >= Five year	0.0159	0.0091	0.0927 **	0.0593	0.0729	0.0791	0.0805	0.0855 *	0.1157	0.0861	0.0125	0.0277	0.0228
Log Likelihood	-584.9	-662.5	-561.8	-328.8	-505.8	-597.7	-660.9	-708.4	-416.7	-339.3	-315.9	-348.5	-410.6
Number of Observations	866	897	713	413	607	717	781	843	495	377	341	375	428
Akaike Information Criteria	1289.8	1445.0	1243.6	777.6	1131.6	1315.4	1441.8	1536.8	953.4	798.5	751.7	816.9	941.3
Pseudo R squared	0.090	0.222	0.170	0.195	0.162	0.159	0.144	0.145	0.172	0.121	0.102	0.103	0.078

Significance at 1%, 5% and 10% levels are indicated by ***, **, and * asterisks, respectively.

47

Table 7
Multinomial Logit Regressions of Determinants of Bank State: Remain a Problem versus Failure
Estimation Period (Years)

Explanatory Variables	1990	1991	1992	1993	1993-94	1993-95	1993-96	1993-97	1994-98	1995-99	1996-00	1997-01	1998-02
Intercept													
Constant	-1.7037	9.8229 ***	-5.7298	-8.1433	3.4994	1.9090	2.3718	2.9545	11.8183	-4.7010	2.4569	-0.1438	-1.3300
Capital													
Tangible Equity for PCA	0.6653	0.9255	0.6366	-0.0180	-0.1213	0.0157	0.0210	0.0161	1.4656	0.2476	0.0092	0.0247	0.0209
BHC Capital Injections	1.8868	-0.2906	0.5581	0.8628	0.4019	0.2479	0.2982	0.3084	-3.3388	-0.8366	-0.3956	-0.6834	-0.6538 *
External Capital Injections	-0.2729	0.1045	5.0410 **	0.4656	0.9132	1.4138	1.4588	1.4872	-0.9185	-0.3014	-0.1564	-0.1621	-0.1645
Asset Quality													
Loans Past Due 30 to 89 Days	-0.1508 *	-0.1852 *	-0.0386	-0.6301	-0.2901	-0.0618	-0.0480	-0.0389	0.6652 *	0.3108	0.5140	0.1504	0.1100
Loans Past Due 90 Days or More	-0.1451	-0.0449	-0.2691	-0.1211	0.0590	-0.0202	-0.0798	-0.0852	-0.6682	-0.2518	-0.1519	-0.0492	0.0091
Nonaccrual Loans and Leases	-0.0503	-0.0609	-0.2043	-0.5441	-0.4911 ***	-0.4661 ***	-0.5049 ***	-0.5101 ***	-2.9075 ***	-0.5721	-0.3620	-0.2440	-0.2381
Other Real Estate Owned	-0.1520 *	-0.0992	0.3269	0.5932	0.5444 **	0.5269 **	0.5422 **	0.5437 **	7.8727	0.7603	0.1889	0.0840	-0.0439
Allowance for Loan Losses	0.2190	0.4678 **	-0.1398	2.0740	0.6592	0.3662	0.4775	0.4219	3.8584	0.5901	0.8449	0.7692	0.8030
Management													
Efficiency Ratio	-0.0094	-0.0479 **	-0.0088	0.0608	-0.0183	-0.0160	-0.0218	-0.0298	-0.0504	0.0616	0.0153	0.0351	0.0417
Earnings													
Total Interest Income	0.5102	-1.4084 **	0.8538	2.3853	-0.2317	-0.2204	-0.1554	-0.2602	-3.2794	0.3022	0.3374	0.6819	0.9719
Total Noninterest Income	0.0929	-1.6561 ***	0.4092	2.3166 *	0.4836	0.2710	0.2199	0.1216	-2.5602	0.6202	0.2145	0.5437	0.6399
Total Interest Expense	-0.4149	0.7310	-0.8402	-1.6448	0.4186	0.0461	-0.0415	0.0889	-0.4817	-0.5840	-0.6594	-1.1102	-1.3588
Loan-loss Provision	-0.5443 *	-0.2876	0.0509	-0.8631	-0.5969	-0.4833	-0.5775 *	-0.5975 *	0.4569	-0.4709	-0.8459	-0.6286	-0.3183
Loan Chargeoffs	0.5898 *	0.2622	-0.6566 *	0.8309 *	0.5432	0.6234	0.5602	0.5720	1.3316	0.6531	0.6585	0.5533	0.3056
Expenses on Premises	-0.0152	1.0657	-1.8408	-1.8289	-0.4222	-0.9661	-0.7504	-0.6864	-1.6630	-1.7840	-2.0767	-3.3064 *	-3.3969 **
Salaries	-0.4521	1.5279 ***	0.6316	-1.4041	0.2488	0.3225	0.2618	0.3786	8.4899	-0.3599	0.0343	-0.2674	-0.2008
Other Noninterest Expense	0.1244	0.8622 **	-0.4144	-3.9178 **	-1.0867 *	-0.6549	-0.5648	-0.4626	0.1029	-1.0150	-0.5520	-0.6832 *	-0.9796
Liquidity													
Volatile Liabilities	-0.0006	0.0166	0.0404	-0.0821	-0.0456	-0.0061	0.0126	0.0192	-0.3160 *	-0.0456	-0.0169	-0.0090	-0.0073
Loans Plus Securities >= Five years	0.0273	0.0089	0.0877 **	0.0966	0.1024 *	0.1027 **	0.0997 **	0.1050 **	0.1040	0.0777	0.0213	0.0394	0.0348
Log Likelihood	-584.9	-662.5	-561.8	-328.8	-505.8	-597.7	-660.9	-708.4	-416.7	-339.3	-315.9	-348.5	-410.6
Number of Observations	866	897	713	413	607	717	781	843	495	377	341	375	428
Akaike Information Criteria	1289.8	1445.0	1243.6	777.6	1131.6	1315.4	1441.8	1536.8	953.4	798.5	751.7	816.9	941.3
Pseudo R squared	0.090	0.222	0.170	0.195	0.162	0.159	0.144	0.145	0.172	0.121	0.102	0.103	0.078

Significance at 1%, 5% and 10% levels are indicated by ***, **, and * asterisks, respectively.

48

Table 8
Means Ratio: 1990 and 1995–99 Panel
(Percentage of assets)

Variable	Mean	Mean
	1990	1995-99
Capital		
Tangible Equity Capital	5.3409	7.297
Capital Injections:		
From BHC	0.1399	0.2176
Outside	0.1888	0.6267
Asset Quality		
Past-Due Loans (30-89 days)	2.2262	2.5514
Past-Due Loans (90+ days)	0.7964	1.1164
Nonaccruing Loans	2.6136	2.5111
Other Real Estate Owned	2.6808	1.4720
Loan Charge-offs	1.6613	1.7754
Allowance for Loan Loss	1.7465	1.9878
Management		
Efficiency Ratio	93.5429	93.5453
Earnings		
Interest Income	9.6398	8.2684
Noninterest income	1.2205	2.1216
Interest Expense	5.8164	3.4738
Loss Provision	1.6035	1.7133
Salaries	1.9194	2.7150
Expenses on Premises	0.6952	0.8492
Other noninterest expense	2.0764	2.8551
Liquidity		
Volatile Liabilities	14.4676	14.2472
Loans and Sec. > 5 years	65.1021	68.6646

Table 9
Effects of 1 Percentage Point Change
in Selected Variables on Predicted Probability

1990	At Mean	Increase in Loans Past-Due 90 Days to 1.7964%	Increase in Nonaccrual Loans to 3.6136%
Recover	**16.41** %	**12.52** %	**14.29** %
Merge	1.82	1.59	1.55
Remain a problem	80.82	84.74	83.13
Fail	0.95	1.15	1.02

1995--99	At Mean	Increase in Loans Past-Due 90 Days to 2.1164%	Increase in Nonaccrual Loans to 3.5111%
Recover	**43.22** %	**36.45** %	**42.14** %
Merge	6.61	6.53	7.30
Remain a problem	49.93	56.65	50.12
Fail	0.25	0.37	0.45